WHAT EVERY STUDENT SHOULD KNOW ABOUT PREPARING EFFECTIVE ORAL PRESENTATIONS

Martin R. Cox
University of Texas at Austin

PEARSON

Boston   New York   San Francisco
Mexico City   Montreal   Toronto   London   Madrid   Munich   Paris
Hong Kong   Singapore   Tokyo   Cape Town   Sydney

Editor-in-Chief, Communication: Karon Bowers
Series Editorial Assistant: Jenny Lupica
Marketing Manager: Suzan Czajkowski
Production Editor: Won McIntosh
Editorial Production Service: WestWords, Inc.
Composition Buyer: Linda Cox
Manufacturing Buyer: JoAnne Sweeney
Electronic Composition: WestWords, Inc.
Cover Administrator: Elena Sidorova

For related titles and support materials, visit our online catalog at www.ablongman.com.

Between the time website information is gathered and then published, it is not unusual for some sites to have closed. Also, the transcription of URLs can result in typographical errors. The publisher would appreciate notification where these errors occur so that they may be corrected in subsequent editions.

Cox, Martin.
   What every student should know about preparing effective oral presentations / Martin R. Cox. -- 1st ed.
   p. cm.
  ISBN 0-205-50545-7
  1. Public speaking. 2. Students. I. Title.
PN4192.S78C69 2007
808.5'1—dc22

2006045993

Printed in the United States of America

19   13 14

CONTENTS

PREFACE

The What Every Student Should Know About . . . series is a collection of guidebooks designed to help students with specific topics that are important in a number of different college courses.

What Every Student Should Know About Preparing Effective Oral Presentations is designed to assist the student in preparing for presentations in any course or discipline. The text includes advice on overcoming speech anxiety and dealing with nervousness, building speaker confidence, researching and using supporting materials, using language effectively, organizing the presentation, opening and closing the presentation, using PowerPoint and other visual aids, and delivering an effective speech.

These topics are covered with a primary focus on application rather than theory and pedagogy. As such, this guidebook serves as an important student resource in developing oral presentations and as a supplement for instruction in public speaking, but it will not replace textbooks for courses that are designed to cover the principles of communication and public speaking in more depth.

Acknowledgments

Many people influence any significant work of writing. This text is certainly no different. It is the result of many years of collaboration and learning with both my colleagues and my students. I am indebted to the following individuals, among many others, for their influence on this work: Joanne Gilbert, Dan Modaff, and Chip Wells, who helped me figure out how to put a course packet together in the first place; Roderick Hart, Mark Knapp, and Richard Cherwitz, who nurtured my tendency to "occasionally produce original ideas"; Tracy Anderson, Kent Wayson, Peter Pober, Debbie Simon, Lanny Naeglin, Matthew Whitley, Bonny McDonald, Kris Barnett, and Kristyn Meyer, who have been my idols in so many ways and even at times my partners in crime; Judith Putnam, who single-handedly inspired my passion for communication; and as always the amazing professionals at Allyn & Bacon Publishers, with special thanks to Carol Alper for correcting most of my numerous correctibles, and Karon Bowers, who has become editor of both my work and life. Everything in this text that is any good I learned or pilfered from these people. Any weaknesses belong to me.

This text is dedicated to all of my students, from whom I have learned vastly more than I have taught, and to Aidan—my constant source for giggles and grins. It is also dedicated to Dennis, Jennifer, and Roxie Asbury, for everything.

1

UH OH! I HAVE TO DELIVER A SPEECH!

It has become almost a rite of passage, a nearly universal phenomenon experienced by students everywhere. It is not enough to master the content of your class. You must be prepared at some point in time to deliver an in-class graded *oral presentation,* or speech prepared by the student and presented as part of the course requirements.

Oral proficiency has become increasingly important in our curriculum. Time and time again, corporate advisors demand that our educational institutions prepare students for the demands of the business world, where delivering a speech is both expected and in many cases required. From telephone sales and video conferencing to formal market proposals and projected advertising campaigns, the oral presentation pervades the business environment. Even the interview process is founded on the ability to articulate orally your qualifications as a potential employee.

Yet, despite how much we rely on these oral competencies, the prospect of delivering a formal speech often evokes nervousness and anxiety. It is an often quoted perspective that on surveys designed to delineate people's greatest fears, a dread of public speaking is usually the highest ranking phobia, higher even than death.

It is important that every student knows first and foremost that speaking in public will *not* kill you! For many students, the oral presentation may be the best environment to showcase proficiency in a subject. For others, it would be just fine if the only requirements were a reading assignment and a written test. The speech situation can be stressful, and the resulting anxiety can make it difficult to perform effectively. Understanding your nervousness and where it comes from will help you to move beyond speech apprehension, allowing you to focus on preparing and delivering the best presentation you can.

Understanding Your Nervousness

- Cold sweaty hands
- Perspiration
- Shaky knees
- Muscle tension
- Shortness of breath
- Stomach cramps

These are just a sample of some of the most common symptoms of the nervousness associated with public speaking. Sometimes called *speech anxiety,* and more commonly *stage fright,* there is almost no person immune to nervousness. Some of the greatest actors in the history of stage and cinema offer stories of stage fright that is almost debilitating. In most cases, though, learning how to deal with your nervousness is a key to presenting an effective speech.

Almost all of the physical symptoms of nervousness are the result of a surge in adrenalin. That surge is a biological phenomenon, one that cannot be countered outside of specific medications and relaxation techniques. For some people, the nervousness stimulates the production of a surplus of acid in the stomach. Over time, that surplus acid can result in gastritis, and potentially even ulcers, and must be treated by a medical professional. Often, though, relaxation techniques are more effective in curbing the development of extreme biological conditions.

Tips for Staying Relaxed

- *Breathe properly.* Many symptoms can be countered by remembering to breathe properly. Before beginning the speech, make sure to take two or three full breaths. In everyday conversation, many people take in just enough breath to complete the current thought. Because the conversational setting is informal, nothing prohibits a person from stopping even in mid-sentence to take a breath if needed. During a more formal speech situation, a pause in mid-sentence generally decreases the effectiveness of the language and delivery. During the presentation, be sure to inhale *completely*. Try not to rush your breathing.

- *Stay physically relaxed.* Over the years, I have worked with many students on controlling muscle tension, most of which occurs in the shoulders, neck, and upper arms. Muscle tension in those areas makes the speaker physically uncomfortable and tends to result in stiff or awkward looking gestures. The approach to counter that tension is to make use of "body memory." Before practicing the speech, sit in a fully relaxed position and make a mental note of what the muscles in those potentially tense locations feel like. Compare that to the tension you may experience during practice, especially if you practice the speech in front of other people. Another exercise involves standing in a completely neutral position. Keeping your hips stationary, twist your upper torso from side to side, letting your hands and arms follow the movement of your torso. Then come to a complete stop with your hands and arms at your sides. Again, make a mental note of the way that your muscles feel at that moment. You will begin to recognize muscle tension and make adjustments during your final speech.

- *Eat carefully.* Many problems with stomach cramps and discomfort can be traced to simple dietary choices. As a rule of thumb, spicy foods are not recommended prior to delivering a speech. Additionally, many soft drinks, heavily caffeinated products, and milk products have been identified as contributors to stomach discomfort. Be aware of the way that your body reacts to various dietary contributors, but also remember that the rush of adrenalin and increase in stomach acid may cause reactions to foods that you have never experienced before. Water is the best liquid to consume before speaking.

- *Maintain a positive attitude.* Franklin Delano Roosevelt once noted that "The only thing we have to fear is fear itself." Although he was talking about a national crisis, the adage also applies to oral presentations. Nervousness becomes compounded when the speaker perceives the oral presentation to be a necessarily frightening and uncomfortable experience. Remember that as a student, you are only one of a group of people who share a common task and experience. Generally speaking, your audience will be in the same proverbial boat as you. Your audience will understand the kinds and amount of preparation required for your presentation. Your relationship with the audience is not adversarial or hostile. Also remember that an oral presentation is usually the most efficient and effective way to demonstrate your mastery of a concept. If you can project enjoyment in the process and in the presentation, your speech will be much more effective.

- *Prepare thoroughly.* The most important factor that will affect your ability to control nervousness is preparation. The more that you can practice the speech prior to the time you have to deliver it for an audience, the more comfortable you will be during the speech itself. Practice may not make the presentation perfect, but it will certainly make you better prepared and make the speech as good as it can be. If possible, and if your instructor has available time, try to perform the speech for your evaluator prior to the day you deliver the speech in class. Your instructor may be able to provide some feedback and additional instruction to help you be sure that you have met the requirements for the assignment. If your presentation assignment includes a time requirement, be absolutely sure to practice the speech using a stopwatch to determine the length of the speech.

Ten Common Errors to Avoid

1. *Inappropriate or Distracting Visual Presence.* Although it may seem disagreeable and even silly at some level, the way that we look and the way that we dress affect the way that people per-

ceive us. At a psychological level, we express aspects of our personality in the visual presentation of our selves, but we also assess others based on the characteristics of outward appearance. Be aware of the signals you send based on your choices for attire, hairstyle, jewelry, and so on. For example, good grooming of your hair and clothing sends a message that you took some extra time to prepare yourself for the specific speech situation. Avoid hats or any other facial accoutrements that would distract the audience's attention from your eyes. Be sure that your shirt does not have large letters or distracting slogans or images. Avoid dangling jewelry such as large earring hoops or items with loud or very mixed colors. Even your shoes can distract the audience's visual focus from your performance. Be aware that visual noise can be a detriment to your effectiveness as a communicator.

2. *Awkward or Imbalanced Physical Stance.* In everyday conversation, we have become comfortable shifting our weight onto one or the other leg, and then shifting from side to side as needed. When speaking in a formal setting, however, that stance can leave the impression of someone who is out of control, nervous, or simply imbalanced. Be sure to balance your physical stance, by distributing your weight evenly across both legs. A general rule of thumb is to square your feet evenly below your shoulders. Balancing your physical stance will help you to avoid swaying or thrusting out your hip.

3. *Closed Gestures.* Hands clasped in front of the speaker or gestures that are delivered directly in front of the torso are called *closed* or *blocking* gestures. Usually, clasped gestures are a sign of nervousness, but clasped gestures can also leave the impression that the speaker is unsure of him- or herself, or possibly even hiding something. Work to keep your gestures open. Openness of gesture carries with it a psychology of open-mindedness, and invites the audience into the conversation rather than blocking the audience out.

4. *Overreliance on Notes.* No matter the guidelines for your specific presentation, whether or not notes are allowed, reliance on note cards, outlines, or even a prepared text decreases your effectiveness as a speaker. The ability to connect directly with the audience, especially with your eyes, is crucial for an effective presentation. The better you know your speech, the better

your chances of staying on track with minimal disruption in the flow of the presentation.

5. *Not Looking at the Eyes of Your Audience.* For some speakers, nervousness increases at the very prospect of having to talk directly to other people in a formal setting. To sidestep that nervousness, some speakers work actively *not* to make eye contact with the people in the audience, but rather to look above the audience members' heads. In most presentation settings, there is a relatively small distance between the speaker and the audience, enabling the average audience member to tell when the speaker is making direct eye contact or looking at a spot above the audience. Failure to look directly into the eyes of audience members dramatically reduces the effectiveness of the communication.

6. *Failure to Meet the Time Requirements.* Remember that your presentation will probably have a set time limit, with a maximum allowable time and possibly even a minimum amount of time available. Keep in mind that the logistics of a classroom environment require these maximum time limits. If your speech exceeds the maximum time limit, your presentation will take time away from other presentations. If your speech falls below the time requirement, it will not have been developed sufficiently to explore the content as required. Be sure to time yourself prior to the final presentation by practicing with a stopwatch.

7. *Hiding Behind a Lectern.* A lectern is a useful tool for presentations. It enables the speaker to place reference material and notes within easy view, and may include controls for presentation aids and voice amplification. However, a lectern also blocks the speaker from the audience, decreasing the connection between the speaker and listeners. Whenever possible, avoid "hiding" behind the lectern. Use wireless control devices or a handheld or clothing attachable microphone if available.

8. *Mispronunciations.* Nothing is more bothersome to an audience than a speaker's unintentional mispronunciation of everyday words, specialized terms, or names. Always remember to look up the pronunciation and meaning of difficult words. Whenever possible, check the pronunciation of names. If it is not possible, choose your pronunciation carefully and *practice*

saying a difficult name so that it can be articulated with no verbal break.

9. *General Dysfluency. Fluency* refers to the smooth flow of language, devoid of errors or interruptions. A speech that contains the opposite, "general dysfluency," including "ums," "ahs," awkward pauses, misstatements, or lapses in memory, will hinder the effectiveness of both the speaker and the presentation. Practice the speech carefully and work to avoid these verbal interruptions.

10. *Failure to Deal with Unforeseen Circumstances.* It is a near inevitability that something will go wrong during your presentation. Another student will arrive late to the class during your presentation, a multimedia element (such as an overhead or LCD projector lamp) will fail, or you will be forced to sneeze in the middle of an important sentence! You will say a line wrong, skip a sentence, forget a piece of research/support, and so on. Count on an unforeseen circumstance—but do not let the unexpected foil you. If you suffer from a lapse in memory or an interruption, try to get back on track immediately and *without apology.* Always test your technology (preferably in your designated performance space) beforehand, and always have a backup plan.

The best way to avoid all of these errors is to PRACTICE, PRACTICE, PRACTICE, paying careful attention to the details noted previously.

2

BEFORE YOU BEGIN

The Communication Process

If you look around, you will see public speaking everywhere. Your class instructors must perform a brand of public speaking every time they lecture. Television news anchors perform publicly every evening for thousands of viewers. Religious leaders deliver sermons to congregations weekly. Politicians hold press conferences daily. Business executives deliver reports to their departments. Students deliver presentations and summaries in classes or to campus organizations. Public speaking is a part of our everyday lives, a part from which we cannot escape.

Sometimes, you will be called upon to deliver your own presentation. To be effective in this endeavor, you must develop a thorough understanding of the nature and kinds of public speaking, as well as the relationship that exists between a speaker and her/his audience.

Communication at all levels is a multi-directional process. The speaker communicates with an audience at the same time that an audience communicates with a speaker. Communication is a complex set of interrelationships that can be modeled in the following way:

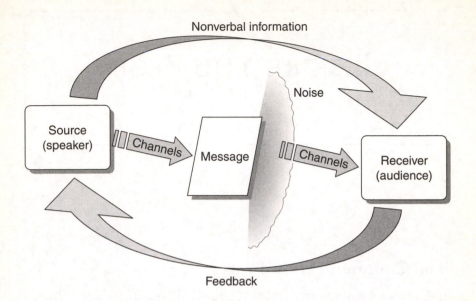

Nonverbal information

Noise

Source (speaker)

Channels

Message

Channels

Receiver (audience)

Feedback

This basic model of communication includes several concepts that should be defined.

Key Concept

Source

The *source* of a communicated message is usually a speaker or writer. The source is the person who creates and delivers the message.

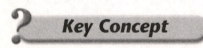

Key Concept

Message

The *message* includes the language and ideas, the "text," delivered to the audience. A speaker encodes ideas into language or symbols that are channeled to the audience. The audience then decodes the message by deciphering the text.

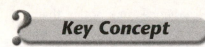

Receiver

The *receiver* of a communicated message is the audience. The audience may be composed of one or more people, and the audience may be perceived or hidden. The receiver decodes an encoded message, attempting to decipher what is meant by a speaker's communication.

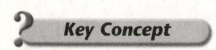

Channels

The message is carried across *channels* to the receiver. These channels may include media (such as television, radio, or newspapers) or may simply include the speaker's voice, which amplifies a message for the audience.

Noise

Often, communication is affected by *noise.* Noise includes anything that alters the communication. Noise may be busy traffic outside of a large window, interference from an air conditioning system, or simply an obnoxious tie that distracts the audience from the message. Noise can be a positive, as well. For example, certain kinds of lighting can enhance the visual effect of the presentation.

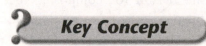

Nonverbal Information

Any information about the source or speaker that the audience notices and uses to make assessments about the source or speaker is called *nonverbal information.* The audience may notice that a speaker is nervous or sweaty, or that she becomes easily tongue-tied. On the other hand, the audience may see that the speaker holds him- or herself with confidence and poise. This information enables the audience to make judgments about the speaker, and is often a source of power for effective speakers. This nonverbal information is also sometimes referred to as *feedforward.*

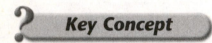

Key Concept

Feedback

Feedback is any non-text information from the audience that the speaker notices. Feedback may include yawning, looks of anger or confusion, applause, or verbal reactions, just to name a few. Effective speakers will make a mental note of feedback and adapt to it wherever possible and convenient.

All of these factors must be accounted for in the communication process. In other words, communication is never uni-directional or one-way. Public speaking is one kind of communication. Whenever you prepare a speech, you should consider the whole range of influences that can affect your communication, beginning with your purpose for speaking.

Determining Your Purpose

Before you can begin the speech writing process, there are a few things that you must consider. Every occasion for speaking has a defined *purpose,* which is simply the reason for composing the speech. *Why* must you speak? The purpose may be to investigate, expose, or inform about a new procedure or method. The purpose may be to persuade an audience to change its beliefs or to motivate the audience to perform a specific action. The purpose may be to convince an audience about an argument, ideology, or opinion, or to refute/debate a claim.

The nature of research and writing will be bounded by the purpose of the speech. More persuasive modes of speaking may require incorporation of more content that is editorial or opinionated in nature. Informative modes may require more objectivity in the tone of your research and written content. The occasion for speaking determines the purpose of your speech. Whether selecting your presentation topic yourself or having the topic assigned by the instructor, you should determine your purpose before beginning your preparation.

Selecting a Topic

Choosing a topic is the first step in preparing your presentation. Topics vary greatly. They may be geared toward persuading the audience to see things in a different light, to change their opinions, to examine their feelings, and so on. Once you have selected the general topic for the speech, think through the subject with the audience in mind. It is essential that you choose a topic that is relevant and important to you, and that you can make relevant and important to your audience.

There are many things to consider when choosing a topic. Here are some questions you should ask yourself when evaluating your topic choices:

1. Is the purpose of the speech clear to me? Does this topic match my purpose for speaking?
2. Do I know what I want to achieve? Can I sufficiently communicate my goals with this topic?
3. Is this topic appropriate for the occasion, audience, and setting?
4. Can I communicate this topic sufficiently within the time allotted?
5. Am I interested in this topic?
6. Will the audience learn something new from my topic?
7. Am I or can I make myself qualified to speak on this topic?
8. Will this topic fulfill the requirements for the assignment?

This list is not exhaustive, but once you have answered these questions for yourself, you should have a clearer idea about the effectiveness of your topic choice. The final choice of topic, though, may need to be adjusted depending upon the availability of information about the topic. Do some general preliminary research on the subject. Take notes. Determine if you will be able to find the appropriate amount of background material for your subject.

Outlining the Speech

Before you begin writing your speech, you will need to put together an outline of your major points as well as of the primary support you plan to use. A speech can be thought of as an oral essay, and every well-structured or well-written essay, regardless of the genre, begins with an outline.

An outline is more than just a skeleton of the speech. Completing the outline will allow you to make sure that you have thought out fully the purpose and direction of your speech. An effective outline also helps to insure clear organization of the speech. Once you have decided the general purpose of the speech, you can select an appropriate organizational pattern. These patterns will be discussed in detail in Chapter 4.

An outline serves three major purposes in the speech preparation process: (1) it enables you to think through your topic and organize your thoughts about your subject, (2) it helps to identify where you are missing crucial pieces of evidence or arguments to support your claims, and (3) it serves as a guide when you begin writing so that you have a direction and don't leave anything important out of the final presentation.

Although the required elements for an outline differ according to preference, the format of an outline is always as follows:

I. Major areas of a speech receive capital Roman numerals.
  A. Sub-areas receive capital letters, and are indented.
    1. Sub-points of areas are numbered and indented.
    2. There can never be a "1" without a "2" or more.
  B. There can never be an "A" without a "B" or more.
II. There can never be one major area without more major areas.

Once you have constructed a preliminary outline, continue your research. As you find and analyze your supporting material, prioritize your information. Be sure to update your outline. The more information you include in your final outline, the easier it will be to sit down and write the speech.

A general rule of thumb is to begin creating your bibliography as part of the outline. Because you will be organizing your support materials on the outline, it is helpful to include the bibliographic information so that you can go back and reference those materials. Including the bibliographic information on the outline also makes it easier when you must transfer the bibliography to a final manuscript, or if you must submit the bibliography as a separate document.

Creating a Bibliography

You should always provide a bibliography along with your outline or typed speech. A bibliography lets your evaluator know exactly the materials from which you have drawn your information, and is a standard element of all academic writing.

When putting your bibliography together, place the entries in alphabetical order according to the author's last name. If a source has multiple authors, then you should use the first name printed on the author line of the publication, and then add the additional names in order as listed in the publication. Publications that do not have an author should be alphabetized by the first major word (excluding *the*'s, *a*'s, etc.) of the title. Following are some examples of proper bibliography entries.

NOTE: The second line of a bibliography entry is always indented.

Books:
Brown, Paul. *The American Political Situation*. 3 vols. Chicago: University of Chicago Press, 1981.
Walters, Kim and Wilson, Robert. *The History of France*. Cambridge: Harvard University Press, 1963.

Articles in Journals and Magazines:
Johnson, Bill. "Interpersonal Communication." *The Journal of Speech Communication,* 43 (November 1972): 462–465.

Thomas, Anne. "Understanding Group Interactions." *Atlantic,*
September 1990, pp 82–91.

Newspapers:
"The Death of the American Auto Industry." *New York
Times,* 14 November 1989, sec. 4, p 16.

Interviews:
Miller, Susan. Capital Insurance Company, Dayton, Ohio.
Personal Interview, 12 June 1992.
Zephalski, Michael. International Business Machines, Austin,
Texas. Telephone interview, 26 July 1992.

Article in an Online Magazine:
Confessore, N. (1999, October 7). Heard It Through the
Grapevine. *Atlantic Unbound.* Retrieved October 19, 1999
from URL: http://www.theatlantic.com/unbound/citation/
wc991007.htm.

Internet Web Site:
Arnett, Bill. (1999, July 31). The Nine Planets: A Multimedia
Tour of the Solar System. Retrieved October 21, 1999 from
URL: http://seds.lpl.arizona.edu/nineplanets/nineplanets/
nineplanets.html.

Use these sample entries as models for your bibliography. For
further guidelines, refer to the *MLA Handbook,* located in the reference section of your library. As a general rule of oral presentations, endnotes and footnotes may also be used to document
bibliographic information. However, please keep in mind that
because presentations are meant to be *heard* and not *read,* appropriate documentation of sources must be included in the actual text
and language of the speech.

Documenting Your Sources

It is essential that you cite the source for any and all materials that
you draw from anyone else, even if you paraphrase. IF YOU DRAW
MATERIAL FROM ANY SOURCE OTHER THAN PERSONAL

EXPERIENCE, YOU MUST CITE THE SOURCE. Failure to cite your sources correctly is a form of plagiarism, and may include substantial academic penalties.

Supporting materials and source citations do nothing but enhance your credibility as a speaker and demonstrate to the audience that you have taken the time to find good research to back up your ideas. If anything that you have to say is valid, chances are more than likely that you can find some research from some source that will back up your opinions. If not, your claims may need to be revised.

When citing evidence, cite the full *date* and *source* of the publication. Where important, include the name of the author and the author's credentials. Authors of books and journal articles tend to have specific credentials that make them experts in the field of study. Those credentials help to strengthen the effectiveness of the information when presented in a speech. Generally, writers of news articles and newspaper columns are not experts in a particular field of research, but are more broadly trained as gatherers of information. Staffwriters for a newspaper gain their credibility and expertise from the publication itself, not from specific credentials gained from studying and researching the subject. For that reason, the staffwriters of newspaper and magazine articles are not included as part of the source citation in a speech (though they must be included in the bibliography). When citing personal or telephone interviews, be sure to include the date of the interview. Here is a quick summary of what to cite in the text of your presentation:

- Periodicals (cite the title and date)
- Books (author, author's credentials, title, and year)
- Polls and Studies (who conducted? when?)
- Stories (general rule: if it was published, indicate where you found it)
- Myths, Historical References (usually no documentation, unless drawn from a source)
- Song Lyrics or Popular Movies (correct title; group or musician if song lyrics)
- Literature/Poetry (title and author)
- Interviews and Personal Correspondence (interviewee, credentials, and date)

Even when information is paraphrased, a source citation must be included in the speech. Any technical information, including facts, dates, statistics, definitions, and processes, that has not been directly observed by the writer must be documented.

In the following example, not a single statement is directly quoted material. However, each idea is documented correctly.

> In his December 1990 Consumer Reports Book, *Health Schemes, Scams, and Frauds,* Dr. Stephen Barrett reports that federal organizations designed to fight against such frauds are not vigorous enough in their efforts. As Dr. Barrett told me in a telephone interview on April 3, 1991, there are literally thousands of reported health scams every month, and federal organizations simply don't have the capability to handle any more than a few of them. The May 21, 1990 issue of *Time* magazine notes that the Federal Trade Commission filed a mere 13 lawsuits against the fraudulent health industry throughout the entire decade of the 1980s. Without protection from the agencies designed to do so, clearly we must learn to protect ourselves.

Some Guidelines to Avoid Plagiarism

Few people intend to plagiarize—but plagiarism can happen unintentionally when you're dealing with the volume of research generally required to construct high quality oral presentations, especially those prepared for an academic setting.

There are two categories of plagiarism. The first is *intentional plagiarism,* whereby the writer deliberately and maliciously submits material either copied from or directly written by another person. Cases of intentional plagiarism are generally rare, but are serious breaches of academic integrity and may carry severe penalties. The second category, *unintentional plagiarism,* is usually the result of poor research organization skills and writing methods. Over time, as you gather research on your subject, you become more of an authority on the subject. However, it is important to track the origin of those ideas. In some cases, specific wording patterns or definitions will be derived from other sources.

Grice and Skinner[1] suggest five simple rules to avoid plagiarism when researching your presentation:

1. Take clear and consistent notes while researching, indicating which words, ideas, examples, and organizational structures belong to which authors.

2. Record complete source citations on each sheet of notes, or write this information on each photocopied or printed article.

3. Clearly indicate in your speech any words, ideas, examples, or organizational structures that are not your own. If you cite a source early in your speech and then use another idea from that author later, you must again give that author credit.

4. When you paraphrase ideas, credit their originator. When paraphrasing, you should use not only your words but also your own language style and thought structure.

5. When in doubt, cite the source.

Consult the policies of your academic institution for more help and guidelines to avoid plagiarism. Ultimately, *you* are responsible for ensuring that you are crediting sources as necessary and crediting the *correct* sources. Ensuring that your source material and citations are accurate is a key element of your success—and is your responsibility.

3

RESEARCH AND SUPPORT MATERIAL

The Research Process

Research can be a daunting task, but you can make your job easier by knowing in advance what types of information you will need. Remember that a speeches is a constantly evolving project; you should be checking for materials periodically to see if you have missed something or if anything new has been published regarding your topic. It is common for speakers to change the thesis of their speeches because of new evidence or comments from perceptive reviewers, so keep an open mind when sorting the information about your topic. Most important: obtain as much information and support as possible. Although much of what you discover will never make it into the final draft of your speech, the evidence will help you understand the issues relevant to your topic and influence your writing process.

Before you attempt to figure out what approach you want to take in your writing, research! Computer indexes (such as Lexis-Nexis, Proquest, Infotrac, and the Modern Language Association [or MLA] database, just to name a few) can be invaluable in retrieving useful current information on your subject, and may be the best starting point. Using these indexes requires brainstorming subject keywords and related terms that might be included in the search functions. For example, if you are researching a speech on civil rights, do not limit your search only to the words *civil rights*. Look up organizations such as the NAACP, the ACLU, and so on.

Look up phrases, words, and acronyms that are directly related to your subject—the results may surprise you. Also, in the articles retrieved for you by these indexes, you will find names and titles of the people who have published information on your topic, or who are included as interview subjects, providing primary information for published articles. Try to contact these primary sources to get updated information. Direct contact with primary sources of information is generally more valuable and more impressive to your evaluator than references to the same information found in searchable databases.

Depending on the nature of the topic, these indexes may not be as helpful. You may need to examine specific books, journals, and academic or scientific periodicals for information on your subject. For example, a presentation on the War of 1812 will probably reference more historical books from the library shelves than indexed periodicals and newspapers found via a computerized search engine.

When you find pertinent research materials, be sure to print out the articles and columns you have found via the research databases, and photocopy relevant sections of print materials. Also remember to write down the necessary bibliographic information. Read the materials in their entirety and mark usable information by underlining passages or placing an asterisk next to longer sections. After reading the entire source document, go back to the beginning and use a pen, pencil, or highlighter to select the material you would like to incorporate in your presentation.

Once you have collected your research, you will need to organize the selected materials. Including the information to be used on your outline will help in this process, and will also indicate to you where there are gaps in information that may require continued research.

Supporting Material

There are two general categories of support material, *hard evidence* and *soft evidence*. Both types of evidence are essential to a successful presentation. Hard evidence provides the logical basis of your speech, and soft evidence makes your speech entertaining and attractive to the listener. A successful speech will aim for an appropriate balance between these elements.

Hard evidence generally refers to information that is factual in nature. It includes numbers, statistics, news reports, historical data, and so forth. Hard evidence fulfills the persuasive strategy of *logos,* the appeal to reason and logic.

Examples of Hard Evidence[2]

- **News Items.** Any source that describes the facts surrounding a current news story may be used to demonstrate the credibility of your argument. These are among the more powerful forms of hard evidence.
- **Expert Testimony/Interviews.** If you or a credible source conducts an interview with an expert in a given field, that testimony can provide strong information for your presentation.
- **Statistics/Studies.** So long as the agency responsible for generating statistics or performing studies is reliable, this evidence offers compelling, quantifiable backing for your ideas.
- **Factual Descriptions.** Virtually any story that is based in factual circumstances may be used to support a claim.
- **Definitions.** Meaning is very important in an oral presentation. Be sure to define technical terms, acronyms, and unfamiliar concepts.
- **Reference Resources.** General research references such as encyclopedias may provide important factual details.
- **Government Documents.** Text documents produced and distributed by government entities tend to be very credible references, especially when detailing government sponsored research or studies dealing with your specific subject.

Soft evidence includes narrative examples, quotations, or humorous anecdotes that support your intent. Soft evidence reinforces your message, displays your unique personality, gives your speech depth, and appeals to the persuasive strategy of *pathos,* the appeal to emotion.

Examples of Soft Evidence[3]

- **Quotations.** Using a direct statement from a famous individual is a good way to show the importance of the topic. However, be certain that the quotation is relevant to the topic and is easy to understand.
- **Narratives.** If you find a light story that is humorous or entertaining, it can be a welcome addition to reinforce a point you are trying to make.
- **Personal Experiences.** Stories drawn from your own life that pertain to the topic can help the audience empathize more with you, the speaker.
- **Analogies and Metaphors.** Comparisons can help to make a point. Although analogies generally are a weak form of pure reasoning, they can be effective in forwarding an argument already well-supported by facts. These types of illustrations must be relevant and should serve a specific persuasive purpose.
- **Historical Examples.** Pertinent parallels or lessons from history can be powerful supporting elements.
- **Hypothetical Situations.** By posing an imaginary story or illustration, a speaker can make audiences ponder the significance of a topic or possible outcomes of a persuasive appeal.
- **Art/Literature/Movies/TV.** References to the arts and popular culture are among the most powerful means of connecting with an audience. These examples also demonstrate personality, intelligence, and humor. Be careful to account for differences in your audience's age and cultural background, as pop culture references mean different things to different people, and may even be unfamiliar to your audience.

Tips for Using the Internet

The Internet has become a necessary and invaluable part of our society, and especially our academic and research culture. Because the Internet makes information almost universally accessible, it has become a tremendously valuable tool for distributing ideas and documents. On the other hand, the ease with which a person can place information on the Internet means that the materials found there must be evaluated with an even more critical eye than that applied to most materials found in published print resources.

There are five primary types of Internet sites in the United States:

1. **Educational (.edu).** Sites maintained by academic institutions, usually colleges and universities.
2. **Commercial (.com).** Sites maintained primarily by for profit institutions and businesses.
3. **Nonprofit Organizations (.org).** Sites maintained primarily for the publication of information by nonprofit institutions such as research organizations and educational groups unconnected to colleges and universities.
4. **Governmental (.gov).** Sites maintained directly by state and national governmental entities.
5. **Military (.mil).** Sites maintained for the various branches of the military.

Most Web sites are connected to organizations that have a determined interest in the information included on the site. Commercial Web sites, for example, are designed specifically to generate business and sell products. As a result, information found on these and almost all Web sites should be cross-checked for accuracy.

- Can the information be verified by referencing other Internet Web sites or print references?
- Is the Web site ideologically balanced or does it instead purport to represent a specific point of view?
- Does the Web site include date references or copyright information to indicate the recency of the information?
- Is the information written well and devoid of spelling and grammar errors?
- Does the Web site include a link to contact the author and can the author verify the information via e-mail or even telephone interview?

Citing Web sites in a speech requires some different considerations in comparison to books, newspapers, and other periodicals. Web sites are identified by their *URL,* or *Uniform Resource Locator.* The URL generally begins with *http://,* which stands for "hypertext transfer protocol." The additional punctuation indicates to a Web browser that the URL is in fact an Internet address to access Web-based information. When citing a Web site, often the title of the site provides enough information for your audience to locate the site. For example, when using information found at http://stats.bls.gov/, your speech can identify the site as the "official Web site for the Bureau of Labor Statistics."

Look for a copyright date, publication date, or date the information was updated. If this information is not included on the Web site, you may be able to find the date of modification by using your browser's "Page Info" or "Properties" menu items. To be fully accurate, however, you may need to contact the Webmaster or page author to verify the dates of the information.

As a last resort, if the information dates cannot be determined accurately using these methods and if the actual date of publication of the Web site cannot be located, or if the Web site is updated and changed daily depending on the daily page views, indicate to the audience the date of access.

Regardless of how the Web site is cited in the speech, be sure to include the full URL and date of access in your bibliography. See Chapter 2 for an example.

4

ORGANIZING YOUR PRESENTATION

The organization that you choose for your presentation depends tremendously on the purpose of the speech. Presentations that are informative in nature differ greatly in both language and structure from speeches that are persuasive in nature. Once the purpose of speaking is clear to you and the research process is well under way, it is time to make some choices about the organization of the speech, based on the chosen purpose.

All presentations begin with some kind of device to gain the attention of the audience (see Chapter 6). The introduction establishes the context and tone of the speech, and generally should end with the thesis statement and preview of the speech.

The Thesis Statement

There is a difference between the general purpose of the speech and the thesis statement. The purpose helps to guide your preparation, determining the general tone and direction of your message. The thesis is a single statement that encapsulates that purpose into a central claim from which the rest of the presentation will emerge.

Examples:

Informative Presentation
Topic: Computers
Purpose: To inform the audience about new advances in computer technology

Possible Thesis: Recent advances in the computer industry have revolutionized the way that we live our daily lives.

Persuasive Presentation
Topic: Computers
Purpose: To persuade the audience to reduce reliance on computers for academic research
Possible Thesis: Though very useful, computerized databases have dramatically affected students' abilities to retain information.

Speech to Demonstrate
Topic: Computers
Purpose: To show the audience how to use the World Wide Web
Possible Thesis: Although sifting through all of the information available on the Internet may seem daunting, the use of Internet search engines can make using the Internet nearly effortless.

The thesis is the single most important sentence in the speech, and should make clear to the audience the overall point of the presentation. The body of the speech should be designed to expand upon that central claim.

The Body of the Speech

The body of the speech comprises the majority of the presentation. It includes all of the information needed to forward your central thesis, including the content of the major ideas, research, and other support materials.

The body of the speech should address the major issues of the speech, including the following major questions:

- What or where is the problem/issue?
- Who is involved?
- Why does it exist?
- Why should your audience care?
- If it is a problem, what can or should be done to solve it?
- What are the implications?

Developing the body of the speech requires that you subdivide major ideas into smaller, more compact units that will allow you to take the audience through the content without overloading your listeners with too much information at once. By and large, most presentations will contain two to three major body areas, with possibly more if absolutely necessary. The reasons for that division are rooted partially in cultural modes of thinking in binaries (on/off; male/female; black/white) and trinities (one-two-three strikes; father/son/spirit Christian precepts; red/blue/yellow primary colors; yes/no/maybe).

The limitation has more to do with psychology and memory. Short-term memory synthesizes knowledge based on meaningful "chunks" of information. The more chunks of information, the less our capacity to remember the information without significant decay or degradation. The members of your audience will retain only the major ideas of the speech, and potentially they will attach some detail to those major ideas, such as specific vocal or visual illustrations, particular modes of proof, or reactions to ideas that are intriguing or that stimulate an emotional response. Determining what that division into two or three major areas will entail depends entirely upon the purpose of the speech.

There are many templates or patterns upon which you may choose to build the structural organization of the speech. In some cases, different strategies from different templates may be employed in the same speech. These templates are not all inclusive, nor will they accommodate each and every specific purpose. They will, however, provide a starting point upon which to build the structure of your presentation.

Patterns of Organization

Chronological Patterns

Arrangement of the speech in a time sequence, usually beginning with the past, exploring the present, and moving toward the future. Chronological patterns may also examine different periods of time, such as major historical events in different time periods. As a method of organizing the macro-structure of a presentation, chronological patterns are best used in informative presentations, but may serve as organizational patterns for specific body areas or sub-areas as well. Chronological patterns also work well for speeches of demonstration or those detailing a sequential process (such as a recipe).

Spatial Patterns

Arrangement of the speech according to position. For example, an informative speech dealing with the development of agriculture in separate major geographical regions. Spatial patterns are also useful in speeches of mechanical demonstration or processes that require the completion of separate stages in different geographical centers (such as a process of textile manufacture), or procedures that require movement in different physical locations (such as a golf swing).

Topical Patterns

Arrangement of the speech by division into sub-topics or classes. Topical arrangements are useful for taking broad concepts or ideas and dividing them into taxonomies. For example, a speech on ethnicity can be topically divided into major ethnic categories. A presentation on learning styles might be divided into the sub-topics of physical learning, aural learning, and visual learning.

Topical patterns are especially useful in informative presentations, but may also be effective in some types of persuasive presentations. For example, separate topical reasons designed to support a central argument or claim, as in:

> *Speech to Persuade*
> Topic: The Fed (Federal Reserve Board)
> Thesis: The Fed is central to keeping the American economy stable, for three reasons:
> I. Because the Fed controls inflation
> II. Because the Fed controls fluctuations in interest rates
> III. Because the Fed makes policy recommendations to the U.S. Congress

Causal Patterns

Causal patterns are investigative in nature and are designed to explain relationships between causes and effects. The causal design is best for speeches that seek to explore a problem and its causes and its effects without the explicit goal of defining solutions or stimulating action by the audience.

Problem/Cause/Solution Design

The problem/cause/solution (PCS) design is a standard model for persuasive appeals. Like causal patterns, the PCS design is investigative in that it connects a relationship between a problem and its underlying causes. The PCS design goes one step further by offering specific solutions that must be accomplished in order to change future outcomes. A variation on this pattern is a division into the cause/effect/solution (CES) design. The CES variation is effective for problems that are broad in nature or simple to define, and that may be covered in sufficient depth in the introduction.

Pro/Con Division

The pro/con division is a topical pattern designed to show both sides of an issue. Pro/con designs are weak templates for persuasive appeals, but are useful in explaining conflicting or controversial perspectives. The pro/con division shows that a speaker understands opposing viewpoints. The pro/con division is informative in nature.

A more persuasive variation of the pro/con division is the concession/assertion division. In this variation, the speaker concedes the perspective of the opposing view, demonstrating that it is understood, and then presents the speaker's own view, asserting why in comparison the speaker's view is preferable. Concession/assertion demonstrates that the speaker understands and respects both points of view, but that a preference should be made.

The Motivated Sequence

There have been many attempts to formulate effective models of motivational speaking. In the 1930s, Alan Monroe introduced an organizational pattern that takes the audience through a prescribed sequence of steps. Based on the problem/cause/solution design, the motivated sequence goes a bit further by setting the audience up for a single action that may help to start the process of change. The pattern prepares the listener for a persuasive message and compels the audience to respond by fulfilling five steps: (1) gaining attention, (2) establishing a need, (3) satisfying the need, (4) visualizing the results, and (5) requesting action.

You will find the elements of the motivated sequence design in most commercials, and the motivated sequence is the basic model for political stump speeches. In addition, the sequence is particularly effective in motivating an audience to respond to common problems.

Step 1: Gaining the Audience's Attention

When delivering a motivated sequence speech, use the attention getting device as a means to establish concern about the topic and interest in the subject. Often, attention is established by offering a startling statistic or narrative, as in the following excerpt from Karon Bowers's 1990 speech on medical testing of women[4]:

> Trapper John, M.D. has long been relegated to the television graveyard, but Pernell Roberts is still trying to diagnose our ills. We've all seen the commercial: Trapper John advising us that a study shows that aspirin can reduce the risk of heart disease. But there's a twist: Trapper—and many real doctors— haven't learned the difference between a man and a woman. You see, the aspirin study was conducted on 22,071 males . . . and it is unknown if females, who compose 52% of the population, respond the same way to the aspirin regimen.

In her speech, Bowers gains the audience's attention by recalling a familiar image—Trapper John—and offering a startling statistic.

Refer to Chapter 6 for more information on grabbing your audience's attention.

Step 2: Establishing a Need

Establishing a need specifically defines the problem and demonstrates that the problem needs to be dealt with. Need can be established by showing that the audience has something to lose or to gain. Need can also be established by showing the audience that they need to be concerned. This is shown in the next excerpt from Bowers's speech:

> While we can chuckle at Trapper's ignorance, few women are laughing. As Representative Patricia Schroeder argued in testimony before the subcommittee on Health and the Environment on June 18, 1990, "Sexism in medical practices is a reality, and for some women, there are fatal consequences." Most medical research considers men the "norm." Women are viewed often as more complicated to study due to hormonal and physiological differences. Unfortunately, the results of this research are being applied to women—without any proof of effectiveness—resulting in potentially dangerous side effects, ineffective treatment, and even death. Moreover, men are missing out on potentially life-saving treatments by this lack of attention to women. The September 24, 1990, edition of *U.S. News and World Report* contends that focusing on the implications of the differences between men and women "would surely prove beneficial to both sexes."

Step 3: Satisfying the Need

The third step of the motivated sequence answers the question "What can be done?" The satisfaction step provides a detailed plan of action for solving the problem. It is not enough, however, to simply make suggestions. You must also demonstrate that there is widespread support or a logical basis for your solution. In other words, you must prove that the solution will really satisfy the problem. In her speech, Bowers suggests specific solutions to her problem, and demonstrates that similar approaches have worked in the past:

> In order to provide these benefits, the medical community must strive to provide testing populations composed of both men and women. We need to apply pressure to the government and medical research organizations to ensure that this occurs. To do this, we must launch grassroots campaigns to illustrate that we are aware of the problem and its damaging

effects and that we will not tolerate further medical ignorance. The January 7, 1991, edition of *The New York Times*
explains that applying pressure has worked. As a result of
inadequate breast cancer research, breast cancer advocacy
groups formed throughout the nation to lobby for changes in
research and legislation—and found that their efforts paid
off. The success of these groups indicates that, by acting
along with government and industry, we can increase the possibility of further and necessary change taking place.

Step 4: Visualizing Results

Monroe postulated that the proposal of a solution was not enough
to motivate the audience to seek change. In the fourth stage of the
motivated sequence, the speaker takes the audience beyond the
solutions, and details what life will look like after the problem has
been solved:

> Only when all medical testing is conducted on both men and
> women equally can we insure that our health care is safe and
> sufficient. When the medical community recognizes the via-
> bility and the necessity of women's participation in all med-
> ical research, we can rest assured that our health and our
> lives are in good hands.

Step 5: Requesting Action

In the final stage of the motivated sequence, the speaker calls the
audience to specific action. Having demonstrated the problem,
offered a means of solving the problem, and visualized how different things could be, the speaker now capitalizes on the heightened
interest by asking for direct action.

> Both the government and private industry need to strive for a
> balanced research population in all medical tests and trials.
> We must also take action to protect ourselves. Until change
> occurs, we must continue to pressure the organizations that
> control our medical treatment. We must also take precautions
> by asking our doctors and pharmacists questions about the
> drugs and tests that are prescribed for us—make sure your
> treatment is right for your gender. Although Trapper John's

limited knowledge about the differences between men and women can be explained easily—he only played a doctor on TV—the ignorance and oversight of the medical community cannot. As biochemist Meira Fields stated in the October 1987 issue of *Omni,* "The sex difference can be a matter of life and death."

Structural Overview of Major Organizational Templates

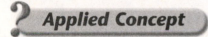

Applied Concept

Speech to Inform

Designed to teach or inform an audience about an unfamiliar concept.

Structure:

1. Introduction
2. Thesis and preview
3. Definition/background of subject
4. Topic 1
5. Topic 2
6. Topic 3
7. Restatement of thesis and summary of main points
8. Conclusion

Often, informative speeches are structured chronologically (past/present/future) or topically (with parallel classifications).

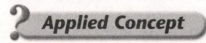

Applied Concept

Speech to Investigate

Best for speeches of explanation or deduction. Also excellent for problems without existing solutions.

Structure:

1. Introduction
2. Thesis and preview
3. Description of the problem/subject

4. Examination of the causes
5. Investigation of the effects
6. Restatement of thesis and summary of main points
7. Conclusion

 **Applied Concept**

Speech to Motivate

Excellent for speeches requiring a single solution to a broad problem. Also ideal for advertising, promotions, sales presentations, and business model proposals.

Structure:

1. Introduction
2. Demonstration of need (we need this)
3. Description of the solution
4. Visualization of the results (see the future for us)
5. Call to action (do this now)

Applied Concept

Speech to Persuade

Designed to persuade the audience to change their actions or opinions about a narrow or controversial problem.

Structure:

1. Introduction
2. Thesis and preview
3. Description of the problem
4. Examination of the causes
5. Suggested solutions
6. Restatement of thesis and structural summary
7. Conclusion

Applied Concept

Speech to Persuade/Argue

Designed to justify the reasoning for a central claim.
Structure:

1. Introduction
2. Thesis and preview
3. First Reason
4. Second Reason
5. Third Reason
6. Restatement of thesis and summary of main points
7. Conclusion

5

Using Language Effectively

Oral Style versus Written Style

Many students write well. The demands of academic language require a continual exploration of complex language and syntax. Those complexities do not serve as well in the oral environment. An oral presentation is an interactive process. It is a conversation with an audience. Though in most presentation formats the audience will not respond verbally, the audience will respond non-verbally, either with evident reactions to the speech (*feedback*) or internal response to the content.

Few people speak conversationally with the same language tone and syntax typical of academic writing. Part of the reason for this is the *immediacy* of the speech situation. Speakers are immediately connected to and associated with the content of the speech.

Writers can create a written text that goes on to live a life of its own. A written text gains life only in the mind of the reader or voice of the performer. Reading a text is a much slower process than hearing a speech. A written text can be scanned quickly, or read slowly and deliberately. In either case, the reader has an opportunity to return to the start of a written passage and read it again.

This is not the case for oral presentations, which usually have set time limits and which proceed at a much faster pace than the reading process. This is the reason why structural clarity, previews, transitions, and reviews are so important to oral presentations. The repetition helps to concretize the ideas for the audience.

It is important to remember that when you write a speech, you must use an oral style. In other words, you must learn to write words as you normally would speak. An oral presentation should come across as natural to the speaker. The more conversational the tone and language of the speech, the easier it will be for the audience to engage and interact with the speaker. There is little room in a speech for grandiloquence and complex sentence structures. Your audience must be able to follow your ideas from sentence to sentence and paragraph to paragraph. Complex elements, such as technical terms and difficult concepts, must be presented and then explained in such a way that listeners can keep pace.

Tips for Effective Language Use

- Define technical terms or complicated concepts in a concise manner.
- Alert your audience to changes in subject matter by incorporating previews, transitions, and recaps.
- Try to write your speech in conversational language. Write your speech as you would talk to a friend.
- Try to simplify sentence structure. Always aim for clarity over complexity.
- Try to make each sentence flow logically from its predecessor.
- Use humor where possible and appropriate.
- Read the text aloud as you complete each section. Make sure that you are comfortable *saying* the text, as well as reading it.

Memorable Language

Avoiding overly complex language is not the same as avoiding *eloquence*. Finding ways to create memorable language is a difficult skill, but certainly an important and even necessary one.

There are many ways to create language that when delivered orally can leave a lasting impression on the audience. John F. Kennedy once said, "Ask not what your country can do for you, but what you can do for your country." This linguistic reversal is a moment of eloquence that will be long remembered. Shakespeare uses a similar strategy in *Hamlet.* "To be, or not to be—that is the question."

Martin Luther King's continuing repetition of the phrase "I have a dream" in his famous speech insured that the audience would remember that key concept. It is nearly impossible, now, to separate the phrase from the historical figure.

Writing devices are useful in creating memorable language. Some of the more popular writing devices used in oral presentations are listed here. These and many more writing concepts are developed in detail in the writing handbooks available in the reference section of your library.

Food for Thought

Assonance	Repetition of the same vowel sounds in nearby words; e.g., "No pain, no gain."
Consonance	Substitution of vowels within words that have the same consonant sounds; e.g., "Do you pine for your pain?"
Alliteration	Repetition of consonant sounds, usually at the beginnings of words; e.g., "Particular products purchased by pushy parents."
Simile	Expressed comparison using *like* or *as;* e.g., "Words are like water."
Hyperbole	Purposeful exaggeration in the service of truth; e.g., "He caved in—it was obviously the boldest thing he could have done."
Allusion	Reference to history, art, literature, theatre, etc.
Imagery	Language that refers to sense experience.
Irony	Purposeful discrepancy between what is stated and what is meant; can be either verbal or situational. Irony should be used sparingly and carefully, because it can muddle the meaning of your text.
Oxymoron	The linking together of two words or concepts customarily regarded as opposites; e.g., "A giant of a microbe; a bacterium with true stature."

One of the best ways to create memorable language in your pre-sentation is to incorporate language that already *is* remembered. Collections of quotations are often divided by subject, and can be referenced quickly and easily. Quotations by famous (and infa-mous) persons are exceptionally useful in reinforcing specific ideas. Quotations can also add color, variety, and vividness to the language of the speech.

6

OPENING AND CLOSING
THE PRESENTATION

The Introduction as the
Vehicle for the Speech

In the fall of 1994, Zina Jacques, an instructor at Milton Academy in Massachusetts, delivered a speech that used the metaphor of a backpack as a vehicle to set up and organize the structure of the speech. The introduction to the speech told of her little boy. After coming home from school one day, the boy knocked over his backpack, and different things spilled forth—everything from crayons to pieces of bubble gum to a pair of tennis shoes. When asked why he never cleaned out his backpack, the boy responded, "Why would I want to? Everything I need I have in my backpack."

Taking her cue from the boy, Jacques suggested that maybe it wasn't such a bad idea to carry around our own backpacks, full of the things we really need to get by. In her backpack, Jacques carried the following items, and she structured her speech around each item: boots (because you have to prepare for what you may step in); a pillow in the shape of a heart (to remind her that there is love in the world); funky glasses (to remind her that she needs to keep a sense of humor); and so forth. The speech was effective, well organized, and left an indelible impression on her audience.

Metaphor is the tool of the orator. Metaphor creates images in the audience's minds that are difficult to forget.

Introductions

Every speech should begin with an effective attention-getting-device (AGD). You must grab your audience's attention. There are many ways to do this. For example, a startling statistic or historical fact may be effective in gaining audience interest, as in this excerpt from William Langford's collegiate national final round informative speech[5]:

> When first introduced in the 1930's & 40's, it was cheap, durable, lightweight, and versatile. Plastic, and its derivatives, found its way into virtually every aspect of our lives. And now in the 90's, plastics are once again taking the forefront in scientific development. What's new with this 40-year-old phenomenon? Shockingly enough—conductivity. According to the June 1990 issue of *Popular Science* magazine, "We have now entered a new era in plastics, an era based upon their electronic properties, and the fruits of the work in that area are just now starting to fall off the research tree." And that tree includes such industrial giants as IBM, Lockheed, Allied Signal, Champlain Cable, and Moltech Corp, just to name a few. Only a few years ago, the suggestion that a plastic could conduct electricity any better than copper or other metals seemed ludicrous. Called conductive polymers, these new plastics have the advantages of being lightweight yet strong, they don't corrode as metal does, and plastic can be used in places that metal will never be able to go.

You may also fully develop your introduction by writing and delivering some kind of narrative or story, giving your audience a chance to see a story unfold and to visualize your words.

For example, in the following excerpt from Karon Bowers's national championship persuasive speech, several mini-narratives are used to capture attention and to establish the mood and point of view for the entire speech[6]:

> "141 men and girls die in (Triangle Shirt) waist factory fire; street strewn with bodies; piles of dead inside," reported the headline of the *New York Times* on March 26, 1911. There was little chance for escape because building laws were not

enforced. Today, we generally view this "ancient history" as a tragedy of the industrial era. Is it? "25 employees die in Hamlet, North Carolina, Imperial Food Products plant fire," reported *Time* magazine on Sept. 16, 1991. There was little chance for escape because many emergency exits were locked. The 11-year-old plant had never been inspected. Unfortunately, this is not unusual. The Jan. 28, 1991, edition of *The Nation* notes, "work kills more people each year than die from AIDS, drugs, or [car accidents]."

Elements of the Introduction

- **Attention-Getting-Device (AGD).** Something to grab the attention of the audience and draw them into your presentation. Some ideas for intros: a story (personal, literary, or real-world), a quotation, a quiz, a list of examples or ideas, song lyrics.
- **Link.** Tying the AGD to the subject of your presentation, clearly identifying the relevance of the opening idea to your topic.
- **Common Ground.** Establishing a relationship between your audience and the subject and even between you and the topic and audience; common ground enables the audience to understand why the subject is or should be important to them.
- **Significance Statement.** A piece of support or research that demonstrates the broader relevance of the subject.
- **Thesis.** Your main idea and stance on the issue in one statement.
- **Preview.** A verbal outline of the speech.
- **Transition into the Body of the Speech.** A sentence that bridges the gap between the introduction and the main text.

Previews and Reviews

Because speeches are primarily oral, and because audiences will remember the most important ideas in the speech, it is important to provide a compact preview of the major ideas. The preview serves as a verbal "table of contents" for the audience, indicating the order of ideas and enabling audience members to track the progress of the speech. The preview should describe clearly the speech's organization and structure (don't leave your audience guessing what you are going to talk about) as well as establish firmly the direction, mood, and stance of the speech. At the end of the main body of the speech, a structural summary reinforces those major ideas, leaving the audience with the most important elements and assisting long-term retention of the content of the presentation.

The introductory preview and the summary can be developed according to the following suggestions.

- **Organization Pattern.** Give the audience the general outline of the speech.
- **Mnemonic Devices.** Aid the listener's ease of memory.
- **Alliteration.** Rely on sound similarities.
- **Anaphora.** Repeat main phrases.

Examples:

- "In the next seven minutes, we will examine the four C's of literary essay writing: classification, close analysis, concession, and criticism." (Mnemonic)
- "There are two variations of the Studentis Sleepidimus, or Lazy Student: first, the princely procrastinator, and second, the felicitous forgetful." (Organization with alliteration)
- "We will examine first, how unemployment harms our state, next, how unemployment harms our businesses, and finally, how unemployment harms us." (Anaphoric organization)

In addition, the preview paragraph should include your thesis statement or, if it has already been stated, should refer back to it. The preview should provide a sense of the range of the speech and should establish firmly the mood and point of view, as in this excerpt from a persuasive speech:

From diet scams to false advertising; from supposed cancer remedies to miracle cures for AIDS, health fraud has become big business in America. Lax product restraints and ambiguities in existing laws regulating health practitioners mean we have to learn to protect ourselves from health fraud, by first examining some popular health fraud schemes, next looking at loopholes in existing laws, and finally discussing some ways to spot and avoid fraudulent health claims and help send health fraud to an early grave.

Conclusions

The conclusion of your presentation is vital to leaving the audience with a strong impression of the text and your ideas. Generally, conclusions refer back to the introduction to complete the story and provide a quick structural summary of the speech to reinforce the main ideas of the speech.

Take a look at the following introduction and its matching conclusion from Matthew Whitley's 1994 national championship informative speech:

Introduction[7]

On June 16, 1993, the *National Enquirer* featured the following articles: Madonna is secretly dating Charles Barkely, a British hairdresser has developed a plastic which can stop the heat of a nuclear bomb, and Angela Lansbury is having terrible marriage problems. If you read this particular issue in the grocery store, or even worse, subscribe, you probably displayed some degree of sense and disregarded these stories as the usual tabloid myth. However, one of these stories is actually true. In fact, the *London Daily Telegraph* of May 1, 1993, reports that retired hairdresser Maurice Ward has done what the collective scientific might of the United States and former Soviet Union has never done: created a product which can withstand the heat of a nuclear explosion. This quiet British hairstylist from Hartlepool is the inventor of *Starlite,* a plastic with incredible properties; foremost among them is the ability to resist extreme heat. This plastic will soon protect the lives of astronauts, firefighters, and the millions of us who look up to them. To learn more about this plastic which the April 18, 1993, *Dallas Morning News* calls a "discovery that nuclear physicists dream of," we must first, illuminate the development and composition of Starlite; next, shed some light on the potential of this substance; and finally, see why future applications are so bright for this remarkable plastic.

Conclusion
Today, we have examined what the British government, with its penchant for understatement, once called "an interesting development." Maurice Ward, once dismissed as a "crank with a plastic bee in his bonnet," has opened the door for incredible possibilities. By looking at how Starlite developed, how it works, and how it will be used in the future, we have witnessed a modern scientific revolution. Madonna may not have a thing for basketball players, and Angela Lansbury's marriage is doing fine, but when the *National Enquirer* wrote that a hairstylist could stop a nuclear bomb, they did more than reveal perhaps the most innovative product of the twentieth century—they actually told the truth.

Whitley's conclusion completes the storyline initialized in the attention-getting-device of the introduction. He summarizes the main points efficiently and effectively, and finishes the text with a sense of complete closure.

Elements of the Conclusion
- Transition from Body Section (general statement about the topic that reemphasizes its importance/relevance)
- Reminder of the Topic/Thesis Statement
- Structural Review
- Link Back to Introduction
- Ending Line (should provide finality and a sense of psychological closure)

7

USING PRESENTATION AIDS

What Are Presentation Aids and Why Use Them?

At times, there will be situations which arise where the text of your presentation will not be enough for the audience to grasp a concept, or where a presentation aid might help to illustrate the ideas more clearly and improve the impact of a piece of information.

For example, an informative speech on a difficult medical procedure has the potential to leave your audience confused. Graphics that show the steps of the procedure and locations of the process would help your audience to visualize the process more clearly.

By the same token, a speech on the types of improvisational jazz could hardly be effective without some audio examples, which would allow your audience to hear the techniques that words simply could not describe.

Presentation aids are visual or audio supplements designed to enhance the written text of the speech. There are many types of aids. A brief description of the major kinds of presentation aids follows.

Types of Visual Aids

- **Objects.** If the presentation is about a particular object, then it is a standard rule that the object should be shown to the audience. A speech about juggling would be remiss if it did not include objects to be juggled. Other objects may be used to illustrate a specific point. A presentation about investing, for example, will draw a noticeable reaction from the audience if a dollar bill is ripped into pieces!

- **Models.** If the object to be presented is too large or unwieldy (or dangerous!) to bring to the presentation, very often a model of the object will work in its place. Models also are effective replacements when the presentation requires historical artifacts or other objects of value.

- **People.** Other people tend to make poor presentation aids, because they can react to circumstances in unusual ways and are difficult to predict. People can sometimes be used effectively, however, in role-play situations. They can also be useful when referenced in the presentation, especially if reminding the audience about a previous presentation or common situation. As a general rule, using immediate audience members as aids for your presentation without asking prior permission should be avoided, because this can make audience members uncomfortable. Also, asking questions that require responses from the audience can sometimes backfire. Be cautious when using these techniques.

- **Drawings.** Drawings and illustrations can serve as effective presentation aids as long as they are carefully produced. A poor drawing will undermine the credibility of the presenter.

- **Photographs.** Photographs are often used as visual support. Be careful with photos, though. Often, photographs can contain too much detail, and may actually distract your audience from the intended focus. Also, photos can be too small for full effectiveness. If you wish to use simple photographs, take the time to have them blown up to a size that enables the entire audience to view them clearly. This can be done economically at most copy centers. Photos can also be effectively presented using computer graphics and LCD projectors.

- **Slides.** With the popularity and availability of computer programs designed specifically for multiple images, projector slide displays are only rarely used these days. Most presentation software packages, such as Microsoft's PowerPoint program, allow much more flexibility in creating "slide" displays for multiple graphic images.

- **Maps.** Maps can be effective for presentations that require a visualization of large geographic spaces. Be careful and selective with maps, though, because they may contain too much detail for the needs of the presentation.
- **Graphs.** Graphs are visual representations of numerical data. There are many graphing programs that do an excellent job of creating digital graphs for use with LCD projectors.
- **Charts.** Charts tend to be extended graphs of numerical data, usually when dealing with large numbers or comparisons of numerical data. Charts (*flow charts*) are also useful in showing directions and organizational details. The major categories of charts include column, bar, line, pie, and scatter. Certain other charts are variations of these basic forms. Examples of the different charts are included at the end of this chapter.
- **Chalkboards and Whiteboards.** These standard classroom items can be helpful for visualizing very quick presentation details. A speaker's use of a chalkboard or whiteboard, however, tends to look less prepared than the display of materials created in advance and in a professional manner. In many presentation environments, a whiteboard also serves as a projection surface for an LCD or overhead projector, and may be the best alternative to a projector screen.
- **Overhead Transparencies.** Although most visual aids can be delivered to the audience using LCD projector technology, there are times when an LCD projector may not be available. Overhead transparency projectors are generally available in all classroom environments, or they may be reserved prior to a presentation for specified use.
- **Audiovisual Aids.** Clips from movies, television programs, commercials, or computer-generated animations are sometimes useful in the presentation, and can generally be delivered using computer resources and an LCD projector.
- **Audio Aids.** Music and other sound recordings (or even live presentations) may be delivered using either computer technology or audio equipment. If audio equipment is not readily available in the presentation space, be sure to bring portable equipment.

Make sure all presentation aids are accessible and clear. Make sure the volume of audio support is loud enough for the entire room. Make sure graphs and charts are neat and readable, even from a distance.

Using Presentation Software

Presentation software such as Microsoft's PowerPoint can provide most of the necessary audio and visual aids for virtually any speech situation. Presentation software enables you to include individual text slides, video clips, audio elements, graphs, charts, photos, digital drawings, and maps, and also enables you to control the timing and display of each element.

Keep in mind, though, that presentation slides are merely a kind of supporting material, and should not make up the presentation itself. Make sure that you choose the content to include on your presentation slides carefully, and that your presentation package does not merely restate what you have included in the text of the presentation.

Presentation slides may be used to reinforce major concepts in a presentation, as in the following slide:

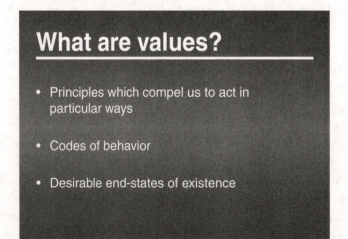

They may also be used to graphically illustrate relationships between ideas, as in:

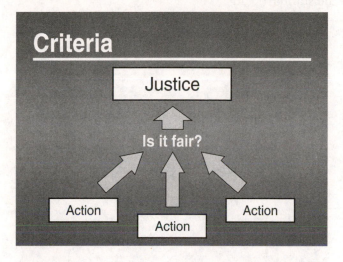

Presentation slides are also excellent for displaying photos and drawings along with text:

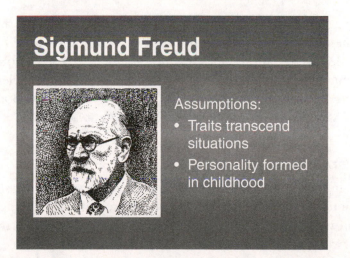

Font Size

When constructing slides in programs like PowerPoint, the software will give you a tremendous range of font, color, and movement controls. Each slide is designed to take up the full space of a viewscreen, and the use of text should be tailored to the available space. The example below shows a range of font sizes in proportion to the standard slide:

Notice that as the font size falls below 24 point, the text becomes almost insignificant in proportion to the space. As a general rule, presentation slides are not useful for large amounts of text, but rather for illustrating key concepts or graphical elements. Major text on an individual slide should be in the 32–40 point size range. Minor text should be in the 24–30 point size range.

Backgrounds and Text Color

Choosing an appropriate scheme for the backgrounds of slides is crucial to the overall effectiveness of the presentation package. It is helpful when slides follow an overall theme or pattern so that the slides work together. PowerPoint offers a number of preexisting background schemes that may be helpful. Your choice of background schemes will depend on the kinds of material you intend to include and the presentation space.

For presentation spaces with low lighting, or where the main room lighting will be dimmed, darker background schemes with lighter text elements tend to stand out better. For spaces where lighting will not be dimmed or where the lighting is bright, very light backgrounds with dark text are preferred. If the lighting in the performance space can be controlled, try to avoid or significantly reduce fluorescent lighting. Because fluorescent lighting reduces shadow and brightens certain colors, it also has a tendency to wash out displays from LCD and overhead projectors.

Layout and Design

The more familiar you are with the manipulation of graphics and text, the easier putting together your PowerPoint presentation will be. Pay careful attention to the use of space, and work to incorporate visual elements that enhance the visual aspects of the presentation slides. The more professional your project appears, the more credibility you will have as the presenter. PowerPoint comes with templates, "wizards" (guided layouts), and substantial help functions that can get you up and running quickly. In the end, layout and design reflect the choices of the presenter and communicate much to the audience about what you think is important about the topic.

The more you use PowerPoint and its related software packages, the more you will become comfortable with the programs, and the more you will find how much these packages can do. You can find additional materials to assist you with layout and design by referencing Microsoft's official Web site, at www.microsoft.com.

Delivery for Presentation Software

Although the major concepts regarding general delivery are covered in Chapter 8, the use of presentation software requires some special consideration. Presentation software will determine in many cases where the viewpoint of the audience will be focused. In most presentation environments, the LCD projector or direct video screen will be located in the center of the natural viewing perspective of the audience. Be aware of the sightlines for the display, and be sure to plan your placement accordingly. Avoid presenting your materials awash in the light of the projector. Standing in the path of the projection washes out the presenter with the light display and creates large shadows on the projection surface.

There may be occasions when the projector is mounted with a fixed display to the side of the presentation space. This may require an adjustment of your placement as the presenter, and in some cases may require an adjustment of the audience placement. These considerations should be planned in advance.

If possible, arrange for the use of a wireless control device, such as a wireless mouse or slide controller. Wireless controls enable the presenter to move about freely rather than being limited to presentation within easy reach of the computer housing the presentation software. This is especially important in larger viewing areas where the controlling computer system may be well out of the range of the performance space.

Be sure to practice with the finalized presentation file several times prior to delivery in front of an audience. Different software packages may handle the appearance of text elements and slide transitions in different ways. There is a difference in the display of the items when editing them in "author" mode and presenting them in "show" mode, where text items may be preprogrammed to "fly" in from the top, bottom, or sides of the display; "wipe" down into existence; or to "zoom" into place. If these text controls are used, be sure to specify the sequencing of the control instructions for each element carefully so that text items do not appear out of the correct order. It is tempting to use many of these "zoom" and "fly" functions, among many other available animation options, during your final presentation. Select these text controls carefully. Animations are useful in masking text that you do not wish revealed yet and in adding additional visual movement and variety to maintain the audience's interest. Overuse of these control techniques, however, can be distracting and even counter-productive to the message.

Remember also to pay attention to the presentation slides as you change them during the actual performance. Often, a speaker will accidentally push a control button twice, and the visual display will move ahead or fall behind the intended moment. Also be sure to build "blank" slides into your presentation file so that you can bring the audience's attention back to you during the presentation.

It can be difficult to keep the audience's attention on track and moving to the next subject if the previous slide remains on the viewer, or if the next slide becomes visible prior to the moment when the support is intended.

If the presentation will be prepared to the point where your computer file must operate without your controlling it, use the "Rehearse Timing" function (in PowerPoint) to prerecord the timing of text elements and slide transitions. Using this valuable function will allow you to focus on your message and other delivery elements without having to manipulate the presentation file. Presetting the timings, however, will also hinder you from making adjustments if the pace of the display and the pace of the oral presentation timing get off-track.

Your Backup Plan

It is an old adage that if something can go wrong, it probably will. You never know when the material you thought you had prepared will somehow become absent at the moment that you need to use it. When using presentation software, make sure that you have a backup plan! Some steps to take prior to the presentation include:

- Ensure that your technology needs are arranged in advance.
- Be sure that the computer systems used to produce and display the presentation software are compatible.
- Be sure that the required software or a compatible substitute is available on the technology that you will use.
- If you will operate from your own laptop computer system, be sure to review the procedures for setting up and connecting to display devices in advance of the presentation.
- Rehearse the use and timing of the presentation file before the presentation, preferably many times.
- Back up your presentation files regularly and bring a backup with you. Saving your presentation files by writing them to a compact disk (CD) or digital video disk (DVD), or to a Universal Serial Bus (USB) portable drive (such as a "Jump-Drive") can be the backup plan that saves you if something goes wrong at the time of the presentation.

Tips for Using Presentation Aids

Ask yourself the following questions as you prepare your audio or visual aids:

- Are visual elements large enough to be seen clearly by everyone?
- Is the aid necessary to understanding the idea or is it merely distracting?
- Will I give the audience enough time to carefully examine the aid?
- Can I avoid distraction by keeping the aid out of sight when not in use?
- Can I avoid making the aid the most important aspect of the speech?
- Is the aid redundant (i.e., does it simply restate phrases or analogies you've already made clear)?
- Have I practiced using the aid so that its presentation will be smooth, natural, and comfortable?
- Have I arranged for the use of any special equipment?
- If something goes wrong, have I planned my escape route?
- Will I have all materials close at hand during the speech (walking extreme distances to retrieve aids is distracting and leaves a disorderly impression)?
- If I will need assistance, have I planned for it in advance?
- Does the aid help my audience to understand and retain my message?

Chart Types

What follows are four different graphical charts of the data:

Ages	Number
18	1200
19	1400
20	1100
21	1200
22	275
23	242

Column Chart:

Bar Chart:

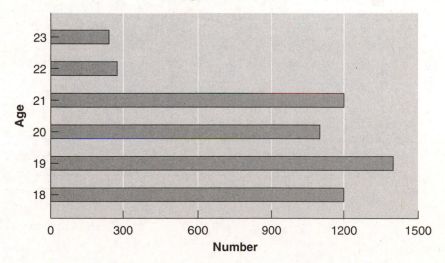

Pie Chart:

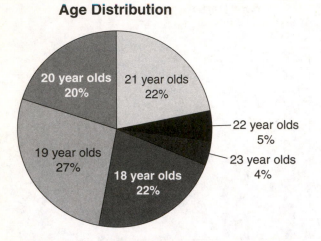

Line Chart:

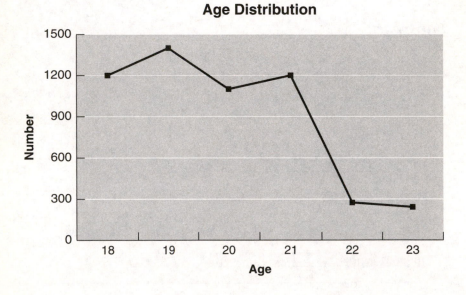

8

DELIVERING AN
EFFECTIVE SPEECH

Delivery can be defined as the actual presentation of the message to an audience via the communication channels, including all of the speaker's vocal, physical, and supporting elements. No matter how well a presentation is written and prepared, and no matter how professional the supporting materials, a presentation that is not delivered effectively will not be well received. Although delivery has no effect on the quality and effectiveness of the *content* of your presentation, delivery has a dramatic impact on the effectiveness of the presentation as *performed* for the audience.

Review Chapter 1 and Ten Common Errors to Avoid for additional guidelines on effective delivery. The following suggestions will help you to deliver your presentation with comfort and effectiveness.[8]

Beginning

Your presentation begins long before you begin speaking. Walk to the front of the room with confidence. Know what the audience sees, and try to center yourself within the audience's field of view. Smile. Look around your audience to be sure that you have every person's attention. Take a breath and then begin your presentation.

Vocal Style

Vary your speaking patterns. Speeches can be made infinitely more interesting by varying inflection, tone, volume, pacing, and so on. Good *articulation* (word clarity) and *enunciation* (word crispness) make everything easier to understand. Blurring words and sentences together makes speeches not only unclear, but also boring. Work to make each word both clear and crisp without sounding artificial. Audiences are turned off by people who sound fake or over-rehearsed, because the vocal style can sound insincere or condescending.

Speak with a conversational style. This sounds so simple, but for many speakers "conversationality" is difficult. Speak *to* your audience, not just *toward* them. An oral presentation is interactive in nature—it requires each audience member to feel and function as a participant in a conversation rather than a spectator to a fixed diatribe.

Eye Contact

Maintain eye contact. Eye contact is incredibly important for making personal connections to the audience. Make sure *not* to focus your eyes on the walls, floor, or ceiling. Look at individual people in your audience, and deliver complete ideas to each person before you move to someone else. Vary the places and times you look at your audience members. Remember that audience members can tell when you are not looking at their eyes.

Volume

Project your voice. Adjust to the size of the room (if possible, test the acoustics of the room before the presentation). During the speech, adjust to air conditioners, mowers outside the window, and other sources of noise. If you are unsure about the appropriate volume level, err on the side of a slightly higher volume. If the room has an echo, work to enunciate your syllables even more clearly and effectively.

Rate

Speak at a pleasing rate. Rushing through the presentation will annoy the audience and make it difficult for audience members to follow the text. Remember that your thinking process is faster than your audience's listening process, and that because of adrenalin, you will probably be more energized during your presentation than during everyday conversation. This requires an adjustment. The presentation should sound a touch slow to you while you are speaking. Recording yourself during practice will help you to identify the appropriate rate of delivery.

Gestures

Be aware of your gestures. Gestures have an enormous impact on the audience and the speech. Too many, too little, too big, or too weak gestures look unnatural and can make a speaker difficult to watch. When not gesturing, relax your arms at your sides comfortably (this is called the neutral position). Try not to gesture at all times throughout the presentation—there should be portions of the speech during which the audience can focus squarely on your face and eyes rather than your limbs. Be selective, spontaneous, and relaxed. Videotaping and watching yourself is the best way to gain a clear impression of what your body looks like to an audience.

Text Movement

Make transitions evident to the listener. It is important for you to move the audience along in the speech. You can accomplish this by slowing down and emphasizing the ends of thoughts/paragraphs and by using physical shifts, such as movement from one space to another, to your textual advantage.

Posture

Be aware of the nonverbal signals you are sending. Maintain good posture while you are speaking. Avoid rocking, swaying, placing your hands behind your back (hidden gestures), and clasping them in front of you (blocking gestures). Be aware of nervous habits or natural defense mechanisms that may result in playing with hair, shifting weight to one leg or the other, tapping feet, pacing from side-to-side, and so forth. Again, videotaping yourself is the best way to determine if your posture and physical characteristics requires conscious adjustment during the presentation.

Facial Expression

Have fun! You must speak with confidence, passion, and interest, and those characteristics should be evident in your facial expressions. If you don't look like you are enjoying yourself, the audience will have a difficult time enjoying what you have to say.

Ending

Hold the last moment of your speech. After your last sentence, pause for a second before you leave the performance space. Don't throw away the ending of the presentation with a muttered "thank you" and a rush back to your chair. Hold the moment for 2–3 seconds. Remember, this is your audience's last impression of you.

Modes of Delivery

A *mode* is a particular form or variety of functioning. Delivery can be achieved in one of several different modes, including *impromptu* mode, *manuscript* mode, *extemporaneous* mode, and *memorized* mode.

Impromptu

To say that a presentation is delivered in an *impromptu* mode is to indicate that the speech is delivered with very little or no advance preparation. The impromptu mode is not recommended for formal presentations, where advance preparation is a key element of effectiveness. However, the impromptu mode is useful for question and answer periods following a presentation.

Manuscript

When the presentation is read verbatim from a written text, it is referred to as *manuscript* mode. Speakers who present the final performance reading from a manuscript, or more often a teleprompter, are not reliant upon memory for the presentation. As a result, manuscript mode enables the speaker to focus on elements of oral performance. This mode can be found in widespread use among television news anchors and national political figures, but is also a generally accepted mode of delivery for the presentation of scholarly research papers at conventions and workshops.

Extemporaneous

The *extemporaneous* mode is the most common form of delivery. This mode is the predominant delivery mode for the business environment, lectures, and informal presentation settings, and is perhaps most visible among television news reporters who generally have limited time to prepare reports from the field, but who must record those reports on video at the scene of the news.

At its most basic level, the term *extemporaneous* refers simply to a speech delivered without notes or a written text. In practice, this mode refers to presentations that have been planned out in detail, including outlines, structural choices, and research/supporting materials, but that have not been written out in final manuscript form. Many speakers using this mode will operate from a presentation outline or from hand-held notes or note cards.

Many students are comfortable extemporizing their presentations. Unlike the impromptu mode, however, extemporaneous presentations are practiced in advance, although not to the degree of the memorized mode. One of the pitfalls of the extemporaneous mode is that, because text language is not fully prepared in advance, weaknesses in grammar or word choice that are prevalent in informal conversation may accidentally be incorporated in the presentation. Another pitfall is a high degree of dysfluency due to lapses in language creation—a variation of "writer's block" for the extemporaneous speaker. Advance practice is the key to avoiding these pitfalls.

The strength of the extemporaneous mode is that it enables the speaker to compose the text and make language adjustments during the presentation, making the presentation of the text generally more conversational. Those adjustments are also useful in adapting to audience reactions and to variations in the timing and flow of the presentation.

Memorized

You may only rarely be called upon to memorize the complete text of your presentation. For students who engage in speech competitions and oratorical contests, the *memorized* mode is standard practice. For most presentations, some combination of extemporaneous and memorized modes will be your preferred strategy.

There is no great secret to memorization, and it is really a matter of determining how you learn and retain information best. It should come as no surprise that everyone memorizes speeches differently. Here are some suggestions that have worked for many of my students in the past:

- Stand up while you memorize. This method helps you experience the speech from the position in which you will be speaking.
- Speak out loud. The majority of people memorize better when they hear the speech as well as read it.
- Try to memorize by visualizing the placement of the words as they are situated on the manuscript page.
- Many people like to highlight any sentences that are giving them trouble so that they can visualize these sentences while speaking.
- Try compounding sentences. Memorize one sentence, then add the next, then the next, and so forth.
- Also try compounding paragraphs. Memorize one entire paragraph, then add the next, then the next, and so forth.
- Tape yourself and play it back. Again, hearing the speech helps many people memorize better.
- Have someone prompt you as you practice.
- Start early! The sooner you get your presentation committed to memory, the more that you can practice the details of the speech and gain comfort with the timing of both the language and the support materials. Don't wait until the last minute. Remember that repetition is the key to memorization.

As a last resort, the following routine has proven successful with a number of my students who had to memorize complete presentations in a very short period of time: (1) read your speech word for word into a recording device, (2) rewind the recording, and (3) listen to the speech, look at the speech, and say the speech all at the same time. Repeat steps 2 and 3 for as long as it takes. This method capitalizes on multiple learning styles simultaneously (aural, visual, oral).

Evaluating Your Speech

You are the best judge of your effectiveness when determining how well you completed your graded assignment. Unfortunately, though, in the end you are not the person who will assign your grade. In the overall scheme of things, many elements of your performance may be evaluated by your instructor. The following is a summary of some of the most common presentation elements that may affect your final appraisal:

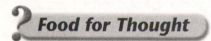

Topic
Was there a clear and effective introduction to the subject?
Was the purpose of the speech clear to me?
Was the subject clear to me?
Was the subject interesting/appropriate?

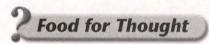

Content
Was each main point fully developed and supported?
Did the speaker use appropriate language and correct grammar?
Did the speaker cite outside research or materials?
Did the speaker meet all required guidelines for the presentation?

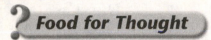 **Food for Thought**

Structure

Did the speech progress in a logical/consistent manner?
Were there adequate signposts (previews/transition statements)?
Was there a balance of time spent on each major area?
Were any areas underdeveloped or incomplete?

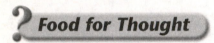 **Food for Thought**

Physical Delivery

Did the speaker seem in control of body and gestures?
Did the speaker seem comfortable?
Was there appropriate physical movement?
Did the speaker maintain appropriate eye contact with the audience?
Was the speech delivered with poise and confidence?

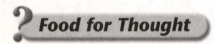 **Food for Thought**

Vocal Delivery

Was the speech delivered conversationally?
Did the speaker maintain control over rate, pitch, and volume?
Were there few or many vocal distractions (ums, ahs, etc.)?

Example Informative Speech: Zoological Subjects

Olfactory Detection in Trained Animals, by Frank Rivera[9]

They killed the dogs and ate the cats. They bit the ladies and hid in their husbands' Sunday hats. For too long, the people of Hamelin had been terrorized by rats. Rats in the houses, rats in the churches, rats kicking the bats out of their belfries, and the townspeople weren't happy. A talented musician moseyed into town with his instrument and played a tune so irresistible to the vermin that they couldn't help but form a freaky line dance and scurry out of town. In Robert Browning's poetic classic, the Pied Piper led the rats out of Hamelin. But given recent advancements, it would appear that instead of being led by their little rat ears to the sound of music, we will be following their noses to solve some major world problems.

According to the *BBC News* broadcast of March 1, 2004, scientists at the Belgian research center APOPO—a Flemish acronym for Anti-Personnel Mines Demining Product Development—have coined the term "olfactory detection" and are training giant South African pouched rats to use their sense of smell to be landmine removers and tuberculosis diag-"nosers." And they're good. So good, in fact, that Bart Weetjens, the director of APOPO, stated that the furry little critters "use their sense of smell to be quicker, cheaper, easier to train, and more successful" than their human counterparts. So, to better understand why in the next few years we will be seeing persuasions about outsourcing to the animal kingdom, we must first, understand what olfactory detection actually is; second, look at its current benefits; and finally, outline its drawbacks and potential for the future.

To begin our journey, we must ask ourselves two questions: one, what in the world is a "pied" piper? And two, how are rats' noses creating a new field of study? First, "pied" means foot—he's a piper that walks around—and, second, the power of a rat's nose and how they are trained to use it. In a 2004 report submitted to the World Bank, a researcher for APOPO wrote, "Rats use smell as their primary sense." Hair follicles in the nostrils pick up molecules traveling through the air. These follicles connect to millions of neurons that send messages to the brain to be interpreted as "smell." Rats have twenty times as many nasal follicles, an increased density of neurons, and sensitivity to a wider range of molecules. In fact, just as human wine experts can sniff a glass of vintage and discern what went into the wine's creation, rats can do this with everything. *The Advertiser* of September 27, 2004 details the palette of rats, "When smelling a human's hand, rats can detect the different chemicals that make up hand soap, any moisturizer, even what this same person ate up to two days ago." Simply put, "a rat can smell about 100,000 times better than a human."

But their little wonder noses would be useless to us without training. [*Visual aid of worker feeding rat presented.*] An article from *Flanders* of December 2004 asserts that rats respond well to conditioned responses, and scientists at APOPO have taken Pavlov's approach. After inundating a gauze pad with a scent, such as the smell of TNT, they would have the rats walk towards the gauze and receive a peanut. Once they learned to search for the gauze, the rats would learn to scratch at the ground after detecting the desired chemicals. The entire process takes less than sixty days and $5 a week to feed and care for a rat. [*Visual aid covered.*] As the *South African Sunday Times* of November 28, 2004, states, "Presto! You have a detection device that, literally, works for peanuts."

While the sinister piper led the poor vermin to a lake and forced them to jump in a mass-ratricide, these rats are leading us to new opportunities that don't result in death. The most promising are in development by APOPO and the Pentagon. [*Visual aid of rats detecting mines revealed.*] *The Independent* of March 10, 2005, reports that researchers from APOPO attach "the rats to lengths of rope . . . and send them out across the minefields." When they reach a concentrated scent of TNT, "their little claws become all a twitter." An individual rat is about 80% correct at identifying mines, so three rats are used to assure a nice round, non-explosive 240%. Despite the fact that that is an impossible statistic, three rats are far superior detectors to the 75% success rate of humans. [*Visual aid covered.*]

Because *The National Geographic News* of February 10, 2004, maintains that there are over 110 million landmines strewn across more than seventy countries—many who do not possess the funds to spend $12,000 on human powered equipment—rats present a promising new option. Additionally, *The Japan Economic Newswire* of January 19, 2005, recounts how APOPO is using the rat's sense of smell to sniff out tuberculosis at the impressive success rate of 67%, higher than even a microscope. Furthermore, the previously cited *BBC News* broadcast reveals that a human using a microscope can test around twenty samples of TB a day whereas a rat can diagnose over a hundred samples in thirty minutes.

Considering that the World Health Organization Webpage, updated daily, and last accessed March 10, 2005, states that because one person is infected with the disease every second, tuberculosis presents the most potential to become "the black plague of the next millennia." Finding an easy, effective method of detection—like rats—isn't just important, it's vital. And ironic, seeing as how rats caused the first black plague. While APOPO's actions are somewhat humane, the Pentagon's leave something to be desired. Surprise, surprise. According to the *Sunday Times of London* of September 26, 2004, scientists at the Pentagon are using a rat's innate skill of olfactory detection combined with electrodes implanted in their brains to create a visual image. Through these mini-computers, rats can show researchers what they smell, allowing the detection of humans trapped in buildings destroyed by natural disasters or terrorist bombings. These Franken-rats will be ready for deployment in the Middle East by July 2005.

In the original story of Hamelin, the piper—angered by a lack of payment—led the townspeople's children to the same lake and promptly drowned them, as well. Naughty piper. Now, while our one disadvantage isn't nearly as funny, the future of our furry friends might be serving to save lives. First, there is not enough research in the area. The previously cited *Flanders* states, "The main drawback of this technology is that the chemical processes involved are not yet fully understood." The minefield study is only in the initial stages of inaction while the tuberculosis tests have only been applied to saliva and mucus samples. Eventually, scientists hope to use live human subjects. Before the full potential of olfactory detection can be realized, the scientific community must devote more research to this subject. And to some extent, they have.

Collaboration between different laboratories is allowing for exciting new possibilities for olfactory detection. According to the *BioScience News and Advocate* of March 11, 2005, Dr. John Church of the Erasmus/Wilson Dermatological Research Fund—who has been sharing information and techniques with APOPO since 1999—is developing a new test for bladder cancer, and all it requires is a few months training, a stern voice, and it's-not-bacon-beggin'-strips. Church trained a papillon, a Labrador, three cocker spaniels, and a mutt to use their smelling prowess to sniff their ways into the November 2004 *British Medical Journal,* which states, "There is no doubt that dogs can indeed be trained to recognize cancer." And this unlikely connection between rats and dogs won't stop there.

The *New Scientist* of May 8, 2004 covers the story of researchers for the University of Rome who used these findings to develop an electronic nose. As the article states, "[The research team] hopes [the nose] could lead to the development of a simple breath test for the early detection of lung cancer." The *New York Times* of September 28, 2004, explains that without the previous olfactory studies, or the help of the rats and dogs, this development would simply not have been possible. Yet another example of animals and humans working together in harmony to create a better world. Except the Pentagon. Naughty Pentagon.

So, today, after discussing what olfactory detection is, its currents benefits, and what problems lie in its path to future prominence, it is clear that more study needs to be done in this area. If only the villagers would have kicked the twisted piper out on his tail and kept the rats in Hamelin, they might have kept their children alive and one of science's most promising new contributors. We should learn from their lesson. Rats might seem like beady-eyed, toothy little beasts, but they are leading us to a variety of new possibilities. So, we shouldn't turn up our noses.

Example Persuasive Speech: Legal Codes

Abuse of Eminent Domain, by Stephanie Cagniart[10]

In 1997, Susette Kelo moved to New London, CT, where she bought and renovated a beautiful Victorian home. When her husband was paralyzed in a tragic accident and her job couldn't pay the bills, Susette relied on a second mortgage to make ends meet. But one day, she came home to a sign on her door telling her that she had five months to move out. To convince the pharmaceutical giant Pfizer Corporation to build its massive new research facility in the area, the city promised the company that it would find land on which Pfizer could construct luxury condos for its employees. As Susette laments in the *Journal of Light Construction* of December 2004, "I'm not good enough to live here, yet someone else is." So she and her neighbors took the city to court, but as the November 2004 edition of the *American Spectator* explains, "the Connecticut Supreme Court decided that if a developer comes up with an idea for your property your city likes better than your home, you're out of luck."

Unfortunately, Susette is not the only victim. Known as eminent domain, this practice entitles the government to take the private property of its citizens. Eminent domain is used, the *New York Times* observes on January 30, 2005, to evict people and provide wealthy businesses with cheap land, or sometimes to segregate communities and give the land to people with "lighter skin." A 2004 study by the Institute for Justice found that between 1998 and 2002, 10,000 such incidents occurred—and the practice is accelerating rapidly. To understand why the government can take our land for any reason it wants, we must first, examine the causes behind the growing use of eminent domain, next, explore the consequences of those abuses, and finally, uncover some solutions to keep Big Brother from taking our homes.

The power of eminent domain, found in the Fifth Amendment, allows the government to seize private property for the public's use, as long as the owner is compensated. Historically, it has been used to build roads, schools, and hospitals. Its abuse is a result of three factors: legal endorsement of such abuse, cities' deteriorating financial situations, and victims' inability to defend themselves. In 1954, the Supreme Court ruled if the government is trying to spur economic development—a vague term with no legal definition—it can take someone's land for another person's private use. The October/November 2004 issue of *American Enterprise* explains that at first this new power was used to encourage businesses to invest in and help clean up slums. Fifty years later, *Crain's Detroit Business Journal* observes on August 9, 2004, there are a number of legal precedents on the books for cities to rely on, so judges rarely if ever rule against any use of eminent domain, even when the justification for it is weak.

Cities want to fill their treasuries, and large businesses or upper-class neighborhoods contribute far more tax dollars than poorer people or tax exempt organizations such as churches. Cities use their power to maximize their profit. Take, for example, the city of Norwood, Ohio. To build a profitable new shopping center, the city simply condemned the homes standing in [the] way because some had "small driveways and [were] more than 40 years old." As one resident complains in the January/February 2005 *Mother Jones,* with that definition, "you could [condemn] the White House."

For the victims, going to court is usually not an option. As the *Appraisal Journal* explains in its Summer 2004 edition, the amount by which the government compensates owners for their property usually falls far under market value, and then extra taxes are assessed on the so-called sale. At a time when owners must rebuild their lives, the uncertainty of litigation against parties that have far more available resources discourages most people from putting up a fight.

A practice that should be used only in extreme circumstances is "trashing property rights and threatens our basic freedoms," *Forbes* magazine argues on December 27, 2004. Abusing eminent domain results in a redefinition of property rights and promotes gentrification. When the government targets small businesses and homes, the *Land Use Law Report* warns on August 11, 2004, it sends the message to entrepreneurs that property is a dangerous investment that can be lost without warning. This discourages the development of small businesses vital for job growth and economic development. By threatening them, cities are gambling their long-term stability. The flippancy with which cities use eminent domain is indicative of how serious the problem is.

Willard Eisner learned this the hard way, *Reason* magazine reports in March 2004, when the city of Stockton, CA, took a plot of his land for a development project. Instead of building on the unused land it has purchased, the city demolished his family business and seized all of the land, forcing his family to leave the area where they had lived for generations.

Furthermore, the use of eminent domain to weed out minorities and the underprivileged—a process known as gentrification—violates our civil liberties. Eminent domain is often used as a way to force poorer neighborhoods and businesses to move out and make way for more profitable endeavors for the rich. An all too typical example of this is Prospect Heights, Brooklyn. Two decades ago, the city ignored this crime-ridden, drug-infested neighborhood. So the residents took it upon themselves to reform their community. They were so successful that this former slum now offers great economic prospects for its residents. So, the *New York Times* reports on December 19, 2004, the lower class that struggled to build this community won't reap those benefits. Instead, their land is being seized to build expensive new apartments and a $3.2 billion Nets arena. And the former residents are sentenced to starting over in another crime-ridden, drug-infested neighborhood.

There are several areas in which the abuse of eminent domain can be stopped: the Supreme Court, our cities, and individually. The Supreme Court will issue a ruling on Susette Kelo's case in June. When it does so, it can explicitly reverse its 1954 decision and state that appropriating private property for the public's use, as allowed by the Fifth Amendment, does not protect seizing property for private businesses. If the Court upholds economic development as a reason to use eminent domain, it must narrowly define that term, *Craig's New York Business Journal* comments on January 17, 2005, which would allow courts to more effectively challenge cities abusing the privilege.

Cities also have a responsibility. Residents in economically depressed areas are willing to make some sacrifices to spur development, so cities must work with rather than around them. The

New York Amsterdam News observes on October 7, 2004, that New York City decided against using eminent domain when Columbia University wanted to build over Harlem businesses and homes. Instead, the city hosted a series of discussion between community leaders, which resulted in a compromise that is allowing Columbia to expand without harming the homes and livelihoods of Harlem residents.

Finally, if you or anyone you know are affected by eminent domain, ask why. Have your property independently appraised to ensure just compensation. If you believe that the government is being abusive, Steven Greenhut advises in his 2004 book *Abuse of Power: How the Government Misuses Eminent Domain,* contact the media and publicize your case, which discourages corporations from accepting land obtained through eminent domain. And please, contact the Institute of Justice, at www.ij.org, which specializes in property rights, and often takes eminent domain cases free of charge.

The government has a right to appropriate property for public use, when necessary. But if the land is intended for private hands, no one has the right to take it from you. Having examined the causes for eminent domain abuse, its consequences, and how it can be solved, it is clear that the stakes are high in Susette Kelo's fight. As *Expansion Management* editorializes in its October 2004 edition, Susette and her neighbors are not the only losers in this case. In a country where the government shouldn't be allowed to steal from its citizens, we all lose a share of our freedom.

Example Informative Speech: Developing Technologies

Robotic Exoskeletons, by Rina Shah[11]

Stan Lee's 1960's landmark comic book series Iron Man introduces us to Tony Stark, your typical genius billionaire WWII soldier. After an unexpected explosion damages his heart, Stark is captured, imprisoned, and forced to spend his days making weapons for the Communists. However, in doing so, he was able to use the scrap metal to fashion a body suit that helped him stay alive. This iron exoskeleton had a support system for his injured heart as well as spare blasters and missiles stolen from the enemy. Though saving his life is pretty noteworthy in and of itself, this metal suit also allows him to take on, oh, about 300 guards without breaking a sweat.

Now, while fantastic stories of robotic suits are usually only contained within the pages of your favorite comic book, a group of Berkeley scientists promises to bring them off the pages and into our everyday lives. The *Houston Chronicle* of March 13, 2004 states, "Move over Bionic Man and make room for BLEEX—the Berkeley Lower Extremity Exoskeleton." BLEEX is a real life robotic exoskeleton that provides the wearer with super strength, and may shape the future of rescue teams, the military, physical therapy, and, the *Journal of Robotics Research* of January/February 2005 points out that before long, exoskeletons will be common for everyone—including civilians. But, this isn't just some pipe dream. In fact, according to *Science News* of January 30, 2005, the United States Defense Advanced Research Projects Agency, or DARPA, has given the BLEEX project $50 million and a 5-year contract to help turn people into super-humans. In order to explore this engineering breakthrough, we will first, examine what the robot exoskeleton is and how it works, second, discuss the current status of the BLEEX project, and finally, discover future applications and implications that would make even Iron Man marvel.

Iron Man's suit comes complete with boot blasters for flying and plasma cannons for fighting the reds. While BLEEX may not be quite as elaborate, let's look at its unique structure and its method of functioning. BLEEX, which is part of the Defense Advanced Research Projects Agency, is the first working full-body exoskeleton prototype. This exoskeleton simulates the structure of a person's skeleton, but places it outside the body, allowing a means of external support. The *Ottawa Citizen* of March 11, 2004, reports, "the exoskeleton consists of a pair of mechanical metal leg braces that include a power unit and backpack-like frame," and *Business Wire* of December 6, 2004, states that it is "connected to the user's legs, feet, and hips." This metal frame provides a movement support system and the *Seattle Times* of March 11, 2004, explains that the wearer, or pilot, "needs no joystick, keyboard, or buttons to operate it . . . leaving your hands free for other tasks." While this makes it easier for the pilot to move around, creating the exoskeleton was by no means as simple—thanks to the complexity of human body movements.

The first robot exoskeleton, attempted by General Electric in the 1960's, was never completely turned on, for fear that the massive suit would rip apart the person wearing it. The reason for this is explained by the *Washington Times* of June 24, 2004, when it points out, "all the 'bones' and joints of the exoskeleton have to move the way a real human body moves." The *St. Petersburg Times* of March 11, 2004, reports, "more than 40 sensors and hydraulic mechanisms are constantly calculating how to distribute the weight and create a minimal load for the wearer," and *NewScientist.com* of March 5, 2004, explains, "it moves in concert with the person wearing the exoskeleton. You just push your leg and it moves." Through the use of these sensors, the robot exoskeleton can adapt to the walking habits of anyone, even without training, creating the least amount of strain for that person to bear whether or not they have technical knowledge.

Over the years, Iron Man updated his suit as technology improved and villains got nastier. Likewise, to understand BLEEX's progress, we can examine its current benefits and limitations. Initially, just like Iron Man, BLEEX will offer its wearer extraordinary strength. The *San Diego Union-Tribune* of March 10, 2004, reports that BLEEX has endured numerous lab experiments in which "testers have walked around in the 100-pound exoskeleton plus a 70 pound backpack [and] felt as if they were carrying just five pounds" and the *Daily Record* of March 12, 2004, reports that the exoskeleton can help firefighters, soldiers, and post-disaster rescue crews to carry heavy loads over great distances for hours.

Furthermore, the technology pioneered by BLEEX has paved the way for newer exoskeletons with even more impressive benefits. A similar exoskeleton is speeding up the process of physical therapy. The *Jerusalem Post* of July 4, 2004, states that sensors are used [to] monitor how the patient walks, and the machine adjusts to improve the process. *Physician Law Weekly* of May 19, 2004, tells the story of Chuck Benefield who was thrown from his bike and temporarily paralyzed. But with the exoskeleton, he was able to teach his body to walk again. Benefield goes on to state in *Physician Law Weekly* that with the exoskeleton, "I could walk for hours . . ."

While there are demonstrated benefits, there are also some current limitations. The *East Bay Express* of April 14, 2004, explains, "BLEEX . . . is very good mimicking a person who is walking normally, [but] has a harder time shadowing sudden movements." Because people need the ability to react quickly, it is important that the robot exoskeleton be able to keep up.

However, this problem is not beyond solving. The leader of the BLEEX project, Homayoon Kazerooni, will be releasing BLEEX 2 this summer, and according to *Popular Science* of July 2004, it "should be faster, lighter, and more limber." The only problem that seems to be technologically unsolvable is the limitation of the human body itself. As the previously cited *East Bay Express* asserts, "If you can't do the splits by yourself, an exoskeleton can't do them for you." While the exoskeleton is not able to deal with these problems in the near future, scientists are working within the constraints of the human body to provide extraordinary bounds to ordinary skills.

Iron Man originally created the suit to keep his damaged heart beating, but realized that the suit could do so much more. Similarly, the robot exoskeleton has the potential for vast expansion in the future. The soonest applications are likely to come for rescue teams and soldiers. This technology will aid people who are working in higher risk situations. In addition to strength, the *Albuquerque Tribune* of January 17, 2005, explains that the robot can even be given some autonomy, so that if a person is injured, the exoskeleton can walk them over to the nearest first aid post. Also, this exoskeleton won't just be offered to a limited number of people. According to the *Irish Times* of October 29, 2004, the exoskeleton was featured at the world's first (and only) consumer robotics exposition, which offers consumers the chance to not only see, but also invest in or purchase the cutting edge robotic technology that will soon be as everyday to us as the microprocessor.

Furthermore, in *PC* magazine of May 4, 2004, BLEEX project leader Kazerooni states that the newer model is meant to have changes that would make it suitable for civilians and explains that the building blocks are much like cars. Kazerooni states, "It's the foundation for another mobile platform." Furthermore, we will eventually use the exoskeleton to not only rehabilitate, but to help paralysis victims regain the ability to walk as well. While the exoskeleton has proved to be sufficient in helping for physical therapy, it relies on the hope that the brain will record and reproduce the movements made in physical therapy, but the previously cited *Jerusalem Post* [article] notes that there have been functional improvements for patients with cerebral palsy and Parkinson's, both of which are diseases that keep patients in wheelchairs. This offers the possibility that wheelchairs may one day become obsolete. For the over 2 million Americans that the *US Newswire* of February 2, 2005, states are living with paralysis, that's a hope for which science can finally provide a basis.

The Iron Man, while fictional, showed what the robot exoskeleton could do for us. By examining the structure and functioning, exploring the current status of the project, and investigating its future benefits, we have begun to better understand the fascination with the robot exoskeleton, whether in the mind of the sci-fi geek or in the labs of scientists. Soon enough, the Iron Man could be a reality we see every day, aiding us in defeating everything from paralysis to Communist villains.

Example Informative Speech: Meteorology

Hurricane Mitigation, by Jillian Collum[12]

Unbeknownst to most Americans, in 1984 the United States came under attack from a terrorist group bent on overthrowing our government. Their leader had constructed a machine to create devastating storms. Their goal was clear, and the entire group was committed, well-funded and animated. Fortunately, the Cobra Commander's plan failed thanks to some real American heroes—the GI Joes, who used giant mirrors to absorb the machine's solar power. Though the ability to harness natural phenomena has traditionally been restricted to masked cartoon terrorists, one real-life scientist now believes that he too has discovered how to control the weather. But instead of attacking the United States, he wants to protect it. The *Houston Chronicle* of July 13, 2005, reports that Moshe Alamaro, a visiting researcher in MIT's Department of Earth, Atmospheric and Planetary Sciences, has drafted a plan to fight back against hurricanes. Alamaro's "hurricane mitigation" system calls for creating tropical storms to consume all of the warm ocean water that would normally fuel an approaching hurricane. A January 27, 2006, article from the National Oceanic and Atmospheric Administration's website explains that, in 2005, Hurricanes Katrina, Wilma, Rita and Dennis caused over $120 billion in damages, and took the lives of over 1,400 people. Even more alarming, the *New Scientist* of December 24, 2005 notes that the number of strong hurricanes has almost doubled in the last 35 years. And as global warming further increases water temperatures, we could see even more devastating hurricane seasons in the future. So, in order to understand how Moshe Alamaro plans to protect us from the increasing danger of these storms, we must first, explore how Alamaro's plan works; next, examine how it will be enacted; and finally, discuss the drawbacks and future implications of this new effort to keep deadly storms at bay.

Cobra Commander's evil plans generally took about thirty minutes to carry out. Moshe Alamaro, however, took well over thirty minutes when he first presented his ideas at an April 2005 Weather Modification Association conference. To explore his plan, we'll discuss how hurricanes work, and how Alamaro plans to mitigate them.

Hurricanes are obviously huge, deadly storms, but the *Washington Post* of October 3, 2005, explains that they start out as clusters of regular thunderstorms. These clusters pick up heat and moisture from surface water, which then cools and condenses into clouds and rain, causing the storm to grow larger. This means: the more warm water available to feed the storm, the bigger it will get. According to Canada's *National Post* of August 30, 2005, warm waters have turned recent storms into giants—Katrina was a weak category one hurricane when it passed over southern Florida, but after traveling over the warm waters of the gulf, it grew into a catastrophic category four hurricane almost 400 miles wide.

Just like the GIJoes, Moshe Alamaro plans to neutralize the threat by depriving it of its energy source. His plan is simple: create manmade tropical storms in the paths of approaching hurricanes. Because tropical storms consume the same fuel as hurricanes—warm water—Alamaro believes that placing tropical storms in front of approaching hurricanes would leave the bigger storms with far less fuel. Without this energy, hurricanes won't be able to grow as large. The *Economist Technology Quarterly* of June 11, 2005 likens this to firefighters' practice of lighting small fires in front of approaching wildfires. The small controlled fires consume fuel, leaving the bigger fire with no energy source when it passes over the area. If this principle is applied to hurricanes, residents in hurricane-prone areas will one day experience more tropical storms, but not so many devastating hurricanes.

Just as Cobra Commander had a clear plan for defeating the U.S., Moshe Alamaro has a clear plan for taking on hurricanes. We'll explore his ideas further by examining how and where he plans to create tropical storms.

The *Scripps Howard News Service* reported on June 30, 2005, that Alamaro plans to tow a barge equipped with about twenty jet engines into the path of an oncoming hurricane, then ignite the engines with the jets facing upward. The resulting updrafts would siphon heat from the ocean. This heat and moisture would cool and condense into clouds and rain as it rose, creating a manmade tropical storm that would weaken the hurricane. In a February 24,

2006, personal interview, Moshe Alamaro explained that the 20 jet engines would create approximately 100 tons of thrust. Since a barge can carry 1000 tons, there is no danger of it sinking. Additionally, the previously-cited *Economist* reveals that the costs for this project would be relatively low since jet engines could be retrieved from retired US and Soviet bombers. This would mean that protecting Central America and the southern US would cost less than $1 billion a year, a small price to pay compared to the $120 billion in hurricane damages in 2005 alone.

In his presentation to the Weather Modification Association, Alamaro suggested two ways to carry out his plan. First, barges carrying the jet engines could be dispatched to intercept advancing hurricanes. However, this plan could be logistically difficult since hurricanes can quickly switch course. So, Alamaro also suggested a second plan, which would call for barges to continuously patrol the shoreline during hurricane season. These barges would then create tropical storms to preemptively lower the ocean's temperature in any areas where it may be high. This would mean that when hurricanes did come through an area, they would have less warm water with which to grow. *Popular Science* of October, 2005, reveals that we may begin to see this plan take shape within the next five years.

Because Cobra Commander was so diabolical, the Joes always had to be wary of the next obstacle he was planning for them. Moshe Alamaro knows he too will face challenges, in the form of drawbacks and implications.

Like most events in nature, hurricanes serve a purpose. A November 18, 2005, KVUE News broadcast from Austin, Texas notes that hurricanes serve to redistribute excess heat from the tropics to colder latitudes. This keeps the temperature of our planet balanced and helps sustain life. The *Boston Globe* of September 6, 2005, reports that hurricanes have other beneficial purposes—they refresh waterways, revive dry areas, and bulk up barrier islands with redistributed sand. Also, in his report to the Weather Modification Association, Alamaro cautioned that if the manmade tropical storm gets too close to the target hurricane, there is a small possibility the two could merge, forming an even larger hurricane. So, while Alamaro's plan has the potential to prevent hurricane damage, it could disrupt our environment by eliminating the beneficial aspects of these storms, or it could make a dangerous storm even stronger.

Finally, Alamaro's plan may result in the weaponization of hurricanes. According to the April, 2005, Weather Modification Association report, it may be possible to design the manmade tropical storms to steer the target hurricane in a particular direction. The *Boston Globe* of July 3, 2005 notes that militaries, both cartoon and real, have long dreamed of controlling the weather to gain an edge over their enemies—in fact, during the Vietnam War, the US military sprayed silver iodide on clouds to create rain over the Ho Chi Minh Trail in order to make it muddy and impassable to foes. So, it isn't hard to imagine how militaries, or even terrorist organizations, may be interested in steering hurricanes toward well-populated areas to wreak havoc on their enemies. But while Alamaro's plan does have the potential for harm, it could also be used to save millions of dollars and thousands of lives.

Though Cobra Commander's efforts to create dangerous storms were thwarted, Mother Nature continues to throw deadly disasters our way, meaning that anyone who figures out how to stop them will be a real American hero. After examining how Moshe Alamaro's "hurricane mitigation" plan works, how it will be carried out, and its drawbacks and future implications, we finally know all about this promising new technology. And as the GI Joes taught us, "knowing is half the battle."

ENDNOTES

1. George L. Grice and John F. Skinner, *Mastering Public Speaking*, 6th ed., Boston: Pearson/Allyn & Bacon, 2007, p 32.
2. Adapted from Martin Cox, Karon Bowers, Bonny McDonald, and Matthew Whitley, *The UTNIF Workbook for Students in Original Oratory*, University of Texas National Institute in Forensics, 2002.
3. Adapted from Martin Cox, Karon Bowers, Bonny McDonald, and Matthew Whitley, *The UTNIF Workbook for Students in Original Oratory*, University of Texas National Institute in Forensics, 2002.
4. From Karon Bowers, "Persuasive Speech on Medical Testing among Women," Bradley University, IL, 1991. Text provided courtesy of the author.
5. From William Langford, "Informative Speech: Conductive Polymers," Hastings University, NE, 1991. Text provided courtesy of the author.
6. From Karon Bowers, "Persuasive Speech on Workplace Safety," Bradley University, IL, 1992. Text provided courtesy of the author.
7. From Matthew Whitley, "Informative Speech: Starlite," University of Texas at Austin, 1994. Text provided courtesy of the author.
8. Portions adapted from Martin Cox, Karon Bowers, Bonny McDonald, and Matthew Whitley, *The UTNIF Workbook for Students in Original Oratory*, University of Texas National Institute in Forensics, 2002.
9. From Frank Rivera, "Informative Speech on Olfactory Detection in Trained Animals," University of Texas at Austin, 2005. Text provided courtesy of the author.
10. From Stephanie Cagniart, "Persuasive Speech on Eminent Domain," University of Texas at Austin, 2005. Text provided courtesy of the author.
11. From Rina Shah, "Informative Speech on Robotic Exoskeletons," University of Texas at Austin, 2005. Text provided courtesy of the author.
12. From Jillian Collum, "Informative Speech on Hurricane Mitigation," University of Texas at Austin, 2006. Text provided courtesy of the author.

Additional Titles in the WESSKA (What Every Student Should Know About...) Series:

- What Every Student Should Know About Avoiding Plagiarism (ISBN 0-321-44689-5)
- What Every Student Should Know About Citing Sources with APA Documentation (ISBN 0-205-49923-6)
- What Every Student Should Know About Citing Sources with MLA Documentation (ISBN 0-321-44737-9)
- What Every Student Should Know About Researching Online (ISBN 0-321-44531-7)
- What Every Student Should Know About Practicing Peer Review (ISBN 0-321-44848-0)
- What Every Student Should Know About Preparing Effective Oral Presentations (ISBN 0-205-50545-7)
- What Every Student Should Know About Study Skills (ISBN 0-321-44736-0)
- What Every Student Should Know About Reading Maps, Figures, Photographs, and More (ISBN 0-205-50543-0)